LITERACY AND COMPUTERS:
INSIGHTS FROM RESEARCH

Literacy and Computers:
Insights from Research

Edited by

David Wray

United Kingdom Reading Association

January, 1994

© United Kingdom Reading Association

Editor: David Wray

First published 1994

ISBN 1 897638 03 5

Published by
United Kingdom Reading Association
Warrington Road Primary School
Naylor Road
Widnes
Cheshire
WA8 0BP
United Kingdom

All rights reserved. No part of this publication may be reproduced, stored in a retrieval system, or transmitted in any form or by any means, electronic, mechanical, photocopying or otherwise, without the prior permission of the United Kingdom Reading Association.

British Library Catalogue in Publication.
A catalogue record for this book is available from the British Library.

CONTENTS

Introduction 7
David Wray

Acknowledgements 8

Desk-top publishing in the primary school classroom 9
David Wray and Jane Medwell

Talk and the microcomputer: an investigation in the infant classroom 16
Alison Hill and Ann Browne

Using a TTNS electronic mailbox in a junior class: a case study 23
Elizabeth Wishart

Reading screens: mapping the labyrinth 31
Vivienne Cato, Fiona English and John Trushell

Word processors creating a social context for learning 42
Kristiina Kumpulainen

Computer applications in the identification and remediation of dyslexia 55
Chris Singleton

A review of the use of microcomputer software by teachers supporting pupils experiencing specific learning difficulties 62
Hamid Sepehr and Duncan Harris

Students and hypertext: developing a new literacy for a new reading context 71
Mark A. Horney and Lynne Anderson-Inman

INTRODUCTION

The advent of the microcomputer into educational contexts has inevitably led to a great deal of debate about the ways in which these new 'teaching machines' might most effectively be used. From their initial linking with the mathematics and science curricula, it has rapidly become clear that the use of the computer has profound implications for the language and literacy areas of the curriculum. Computers provide a new medium (or, more accurately, a range of new media) for communication and therefore imply new forms of literacy. They also provide new contexts in which communication of all kinds is used - most educational uses of computers are based around group rather than individual use. As such they provide new challenges for teachers, both conceptually (what are my children actually learning as they use the computer?) and organisationally (how can I best manage this new resource to best effect?) As with all such educational questions, answers are beginning to emerge from accounts of classroom practice and from more systematic attempts to study particular questions.

The papers in this collection include reports stemming from both these approaches, but the major focus of the volume is on the insights into educational computer use which we can gain from research. Here are reported studies of the context provided by computers for children's talk (the papers by Hill & Browne and by Kumpulainen), the new forms of literacy offered by the use of the computer (Wray & Medwell, Wishart), the ways readers approach the new screen-based text presentations (Cato, English & Trushell, Horney & Anderson-Inman), the perceptions and use of computers by groups of teachers (Sepehr & Harris) and the use of computers with children with specific literacy needs (Singleton).

Naturally, the eight papers included here do not provide a definitive set of answers to the many questions which are raised about language and literacy teaching by the new technology. They do, however, make a good series of starting points for teachers' thinking and for further research. They also, I hope, give firm evidence that, in the development of effective ways to use computers to further literacy, research can offer some valuable insights.

Acknowledgements

Three of these chapters were originally published in the journal *Reading*:

Talk and the microcomputer: an investigation in the infant classroom
Alison Hill and Ann Browne

Using a TTNS electronic mailbox in a junior class: a case study
Elizabeth Wishart

Reading screens: mapping the labyrinth
Vivienne Cato, Fiona English and John Trushell

Two papers were presented at the 1992 annual conference of the United Kingdom Reading Association at the University of Exeter:

Computer applications in the identification and remediation of dyslexia ....
Chris Singleton

Students and hypertext: developing a new literacy for a new reading context .....
Mark A. Horney and Lynne Anderson-Inman

The remaining papers were specially written for this volume.

Desk-top Publishing in the Primary School Classroom

David Wray & Jane Medwell

Desk-top publishing: a revolution in the making

The last few years have seen dramatic growth in the use of computer systems for desk-top publishing, that is, the production of books, journals, newspapers etc. by writers themselves, without the intermediate stage of specialist typesetting. These developments have been controversial in that they signal the redundancy of a highly skilled group of workers, typesetters, but this should not mask the real enablement which they imply. Because of the new technology, the production of printed materials to professional standards is suddenly available to anybody with access to a computer, suitable printer and appropriate software. The effects of this revolution have not, as yet, been explored, but cannot help but be significant (Wray, 1989).

The potential of desk-top publishing as a vehicle for the production of children's work has certainly been seen by many primary schools in the United Kingdom. Desk-top publishing has emerged as an enabling device for children. Using presently available hardware such as Acorn A3000 and A5000 computers, ink-jet or laser printers, scanners and digitisers and software such as *Pendown*, *Impression* and *Ovation*, children can produce published work of much higher surface quality than could be achieved using old-fashioned typewriters, scissors and glue. Because the technicalities of production are simpler, children are allowed to devote more of their concentration to the substance of what they wish to produce. A consequent improvement in real quality might, therefore, also be expected.

In this chapter we shall aim to do three things. We shall firstly explore some of the potential which desk-top publishing seems to have for the development of literacy in the primary school. (For a fuller discussion of this, see Wray & Medwell (1989)). Secondly, we shall outline some of the forms it might take. Finally we shall describe some of the classroom strategies which have been employed to introduce desk-top publishing to primary children.

Desk-top publishing: a rationale

Desk-top publishing, as an extension of word-processing, naturally has similar effects upon children's writing. Perhaps the most obvious is that it enables all children to achieve success in the physical appearance of their writing. All writing done on the computer, whatever its quality, 'looks good'. The computer does not allow differentiation between those with well and poorly developed physical writing skills. Word-processed text has a professional physical appearance, and this enables children to stop worrying about this aspect of writing and give more attention to its real aim of effective communication.

This in itself would not, of course, be sufficient reason for encouraging children to use the computer to write. Many teachers have also found (Trushell & Broderick, 1984; Smith, 1986) that word-processing leads to an improved quality in children's writing. Because editing and revising texts can be done so simply on the screen, children are readily persuaded to edit and revise their writing, with consequent improvement in content, style, clarity etc. On the computer all writing becomes provisional, and open to addition, extension, rearrangement, deletion and reshaping. This fact cannot help but have profound implications for children's perceptions of the process of writing and its products.

Desktop publishing goes further than straight word-processing, however, and its additional features make it extremely suitable for use as an educational writing environment. The first of these concerns the purposes for which it is typically used. Perhaps the most common use of desktop publishing is in the production of a class or school newspaper or magazine. This end-product is, by its nature, intended for other people to read, and its producers are therefore involved in 'public' writing, that is, writing for an audience. This fact adds a dimension of purposefulness to writing which children may occasionally not perceive in other writing tasks. The demands of an audience in turn give children greater incentive to improve the quality and accuracy of their writing.

Another feature of the production of newspapers and magazines through desktop publishing is that these media are generally very familiar to children. They recognise their distinctive features and appreciate the facility that desktop publishing gives them of emulating these 'real life' features. Children are often much more aware than might be imagined of the importance of such newspaper features as type-face, design, layout and style of writing. In addition, one of the benefits of using desk-top publishing packages with children is a sharpening of this awareness. Desktop publishing facilitates the production of writing in a variety of formats, from newspaper to story book, each with its own distinct set of conventions. To produce successful documents children have to come to terms with and use these conventions. Thus the use of the software enhances children's literacy awareness.

The desktop publishing environment has some features which make it particularly useful for the production of "realistic" writing, that is writing which fits a real life format. One of the most important of these, which the more elaborate software packages have, is the cut and paste facility. By this, sections of pages can be electronically lifted from one place and moved or copied to another. This facility permits an extension of the concept of provisionality referred to above. Anything children write can always be changed. With word-processing changes are largely limited to content, but with desk-top publishing not only content but format also are provisional. Children can change the documents they are working on in a number of ways, and they quickly grasp the power of this, and experiment with format. This again is likely to increase their awareness of the effects of different formats on their readers, another important literacy skill. They can, of course, experiment with several layouts before finally committing themselves to one. Indeed, they can also easily print out alternative layouts and gain some feedback on their appropriateness and acceptability from other readers. This can only increase their awareness of the demands of different audiences.

Another feature which desktop publishing makes possible is the mixing of text and pictures. In systems which are sophisticated but not beyond the reach of primary schools it is possible for users to snatch pictures from video players and cameras, and import these as digitised pictures into the desktop publishing environment. Once under the control of the computer software, these pictures can be manipulated in various ways: stretched, enlarged, reduced, rotated, reversed, chopped into pieces and overlaid or interspersed with text. This is a facility of immense potential, which, coupled with the use of high quality printers, enables users of small personal computers to produce pages which are almost indistinguishable from those of real newspapers.

It is clear that desktop publishing has a great potential as an environment for the purposeful development and practice of many literacy skills. There are several ways in which it can be used in the classroom, from physical cutting and pasting of word-processed text to the use of sophisticated and dedicated software packages. In some ways it is possible to see this range in terms of a sequential development, allowing for the gradual broadening of children's skills. The next section of this paper will briefly outline some of these techniques and their associated software.

Desk-top publishing techniques

1. Physical cut and paste.

The easiest way to introduce children to the techniques of desk-top publishing is to use physical cut and paste techniques, which many teachers will already have tried at some time. This simply involves cutting out pieces of writing and pictures, arranging these on a large sheet of paper, and sticking them down with adhesive. This procedure can be greatly eased and improved if the writing used is first printed out via a word-processor. This is not just a question of improved neatness, important as this is. A feature of most word-processors is their ability to produce pieces of writing in a variety of formats. Thus a piece could be produced in standard 80 letters per line format, or for a newspaper, for example, in 20 letters a line format. This naturally gives a good deal more flexibility in the preparation of the finished product.

A further dimension which several modern educational word-processing packages give is the ability to print out text in a variety of fonts and sizes, from normal size Roman to giant Gothic. Thus text can be produced in fonts suitable for headlines or even more elaborate purposes, which again gives extra flexibility and potential for experimentation.

2. Newspaper emulations.

There are software packages now available which are deliberately designed to facilitate the production of school newspapers. These range from pre-formatted packages which ask, "What is your newspaper called?", "What is your headline?" etc., to more open-ended packages. What they have in common is the ability to produce boxes on the screen and subsequently on the printout, into which the writers can then stick suitable pictures, photographs etc.

3. Graphics / text mixing packages.

Software is available which allows writers to incorporate graphics into their writing. This may consist of a facility to download pictures from a video and incorporate them into text in whatever form is required. There may also be a facility to use a scanner, that is, a hand-held device which, when passed over photographs or drawings, will copy these into the computer for subsequent working on. Prior to using such devices, children may use word-processing packages with collections of 'clip-art', that is, pre-drawn, cartoon-type pictures stored on a computer disk. The user can select any of these pictures and insert it onto the writing page, which can then be printed out. This then provides a simple way of adding illustrations to writing.

4. Full desk-top publishing packages.

Full desk-top publishing packages tend to be designed for adult use rather than specifically for schools, and consequently are often quite complex to use. We should bear in mind, though, that the trend in computer design is not only to make them more and more powerful, but also more and more simple to use. The features provided by desk-top publishing packages vary, but the user should expect to be able to:
• enter text and reformat it as required,
• select from a variety of fonts and text sizes and mix these on a page,

- load in text previously written on a word-processor,
- place text anywhere on a page, or in a document,
- incorporate pictures into a page, either from a pre-drawn collection, digitised video or scanned pictures.

There are several desk-top publishing packages specially designed for use in primary schools and there can be little doubt that interest in this area will ensure that even more powerful packages will emerge in the near future, helped by improvements in hardware capability. Desk-top publishing has such potential for enabling children that it is undoubtedly here to stay.

In the final section of this chapter we shall outline some classroom strategies which might be employed to successfully introduce desk-top publishing into the primary classroom.

Classroom strategies

1. Use of Computer time.

In view of the financial demands already made on schools it seems likely that many schools will have to struggle on with their inadequate provision of one computer for a number of classes. Teachers will have to use this limited time for other uses in addition to word processing. It is essential, therefore, that this time is put to the best use to allow all children maximum possible experience. One way to make the most of word processing time is to limit the type of writing that is done on the machine. It is possible that all writing would benefit from the use of a computer but, alas, this is unrealistic. It has been suggested (Potter, 1988) that writing which best makes use of the facilities of the word-processor is:
- public (for audiences beyond the teacher),
- non-narrative (reports, persuasive writing etc.),
- short (space and time being precious),
- collaborative (giving several children computer experience at once).

The writing task which meets all of these criteria is the production of a class newspaper and it is no surprise that newspaper work has become perhaps the most widely used aspect of computer usage in primary schools.

2. Class introduction of programs.

When using a new word processing or desk top publishing program it is useful to run a whole class session to introduce the program. The possibilities offered by a new program can be discussed with the class, and usually generate interest and enthusiasm. Following this, groups in the class might sign up for particular projects using the program.

3. Peer tutoring.

A class introduction generates interest, enthusiasm, talk and ideas but is not sufficient introduction to most programs. The effectiveness of peer tutoring has been discussed by Topping (1987) and the introduction of new programs seems to be a good area for this. Following the class discussion a small group of children are chosen to be the class "experts" for this program. This group work on their task under the teacher's supervision. By the time they have completed their task they are familiar with the program and in a position to help other children in the class. When other groups start, they work with the advice of one of the "experts" and teacher intervention is usually unnecessary.

4. Larger Projects.

Having involved children in group work on the word processor, many teachers will go on to use it for a class task such as a guide book or newspaper. When planning a larger project it is important that the children have a certain degree of control, and are involved to the fullest extent possible and this means that the teacher must organise carefully. When groups sign up for larger projects and state what part they wish to do the teacher will need to do some negotiating to ensure the most effective use of individual talents. As part of a larger project the team of "experts" (children familiar with the computer program) can also be editors of the finished product and select the stories, artwork, etc that will appear in the final version. Physically, it is easier to manage a large publication on the word processor if it is organised around an editor's desk holding the computer and all the interviews, tapes, plans, drafts and discs used. These can be organised in deep trays and divided by task sheets so that the teacher can see at a glance how work is progressing.

5. Evaluation.

A very important part of any writing is evaluation, and this is doubly so with word processed work where the program itself may also be scrutinised. To some extent products that meet the criteria for word processing tend to be evaluated by their audience. Posters attract attention, children are interested by a school newspaper, parents comment on a school guidebook, etc. However, teachers aim to develop the critical faculties of each child, and to do that they need to learn to evaluate their own work. A "sharing time" one afternoon each week allows time for this. When several groups have had a chance to use a program they can bring the products (or drafts) to show and discuss; this inevitably leads to discussion of the program. The children can be positively critical of work, and recognise the shortcomings of programs with surprising ease. Children are able to recognise lapses of authenticity in shape and font, and supply some ideas to avoid this. This sort of session not only revives the enthusiasm of those waiting their turn, but also gives feedback from which they can profit.

Conclusion

As we argued at the beginning of this paper, there can be little doubt that desk-top publishing is here to stay as a writing medium and has great potential for primary classrooms. The demands of the National Curriculum in British schools make a place for word-processing and desk-top publishing essential, but even if this were not so, the media are self-evidently useful and important. Many teachers will find innovative ways of using them. It is our hope that this chapter may be a useful starting point for this.

References

Potter, F. (1988) *The word-processor: a new literacy tool.* Paper presented at CEC Summer University on Writing and First Contacts with Written Language, University of Toulouse le Mirail

Smith, B. (1986) "The use of the word-processor with developing writers", in Wray, D. & Potter, F. eds., *Micro-Explorations 2*, United Kingdom Reading Association

Topping K. (1987) *The peer tutoring handbook* Croom Helm: London

Trushell, J. & Broderick, C. (1985) "Primary observations of word - processing", in Potter, F. & Wray, D. eds., *Micro-Explorations 1*, United Kingdom Reading Association

Wray, D. (1989) "Text-processing and literacy", paper presented at the 22nd Annual Conference of the United Kingdom Reading Association, Ormskirk

Wray, D. & Medwell, J. (1989) "Using desk-top publishing to develop literacy", in *Reading,* Vol. 23, No. 2, pp 62-68

Talk and the microcomputer: an investigation in the infant classroom

Alison Hill and Ann Browne

'One of the most striking aspects of the use of the computer in the primary classroom is the amount of talk that is generated' (Schenk, 1984a).

The main aims of this piece of small scale classroom based research were,
(a) to investigate the quantity, quality and distribution of talk generated by the use of a computer program when working with a class of six and seven year old children,
and, (b) to consider some practical implications for the teacher when using computers in the classroom to implement (a) above. Such considerations included the role of the teacher, that is teacher preparation and intervention, pupil group size and group composition, seating arrangements, the length of sessions, the need for match of programme to pupil and programme evaluation.

Much of the writing about computer programs by authors, researchers and reviewers (Bleach, 1984, Fox, 1985) suggests that they have a great deal to offer in fostering talk in the classroom. It has long been acknowledged that talk in its own right is valuable particularly when extended in the classroom (Tough, 1981). But writers about the computer as a generator of talk have not yet given much detailed analysis or description of the quality and nature of discussion that computer programmes promote especially with infant age children. Similarly writers have not given any clear picture of the practical and organisational issues that the use of a computer with infants might involve. Although some attempt has been made to give this information when working with junior age children in the video *Flowers for the Teacher*, (Schenk (1984a) and the MEP project material (1984) are perhaps the most helpful to date giving some indication of the sort of language that computer programmes might promote and some of the practical ways in which computer work can be set up with classes of children. A later MEP Pack (1985) gives an audio tape which provides an example of children's talk whilst working on the program *The Lost Frog*. It is evident from listening to this that the talk generated is plentiful and of a high quality, but again it is not accompanied by detailed analysis. (Fox 1986) and Robinson (1985) give some indication of what might be possible but also make clear that further investigation of the issues outlined at the beginning of this article are needed. 'We have not yet begun to explore the potential of the computer for oral work in schools.' (Robinson, 1985).

It was with this information in mind that a short term piece of research lasting three complete weeks and ten single days was undertaken with a class of thirty two six to seven year olds in a primary school where there was a high degree of interest in promoting the use of its four computers but where no work had yet been done with the infant classes. The program *Granny's Garden* was selected for use since it met some of the author's previously established criteria for an effective program that would sustain interest and work over an extended period. Such criteria included good use of graphics and colour, thorough documentation, clear instructions for both the teacher and the children and the potential to be integrated into other curriculum areas. The nature of the program and its length were sufficient to test the hypothesis that programs can generate discussion and to carry out a full and detailed investigation of the resulting children's talk. It has a number of sections that might promote a variety of talk and provide convenient stopping places for the children. The magical element seemed appropriate for young children and seemed likely to be able to sustain their interest and motivation, something of vital importance if talk was to be generated and analysed. It seemed likely that the program would require children to work both as groups and in groups thus encouraging interaction, co-operation and group decision making.

Having selected the program it was then necessary to select two groups of children to observe and tape record while they worked with the micro-computer. The thirty two children were divided into eight groups of four. Four had been recently identified as the optimum number to work around one micro-computer when talk is the object (Potter, 1985). As far as possible each group included two girls, two boys, two six year olds and two seven year olds. A mix of ability was also taken into account. The two groups selected for particular observation were evenly balanced in terms of personality, sex, age, general ability, ability in reading and skills in co-operation and group interaction. With group A the teacher's role was to give as much help as needed and to teach when appropriate. With group B the teacher's role was that of minimal intervention, leaving the children to work very much on their own and only giving the children as much help as normal classroom organisation would usually allow for any group of children engaged in a group activity. This was also the teacher's role with every other group of four who worked on the computer, the only difference being that only group A's and group B's discussions were tape recorded and analysed.

Since every child in the class was involved in working on *Granny's Garden* as the basis of a short class topic the project began with a whole class introduction to the program. The class were taken through the program up to the stage of entering the woodcutter's cottage thus interesting the children in what was to come. This form of introduction also allowed whole class discussion of the program, something advocated by Schenk (1984b). A poster displaying the main keys of the computer keyboard was prepared, introduced to the children and displayed in the classroom.

To help with written work associated with the program the children were introduced to a word bank containing some of the key words in the program. They were also introduced to the idea of taking notes whilst working at the computer.

After these preliminary organisational issues had been dealt with there were two further considerations, the organisation of seating and the length of sessions on the computer. When considering seating a number of variants were tried. If the keyboard was positioned on a rectangular table this appeared to exclude the children at each end from the group discussion since they were physically more distant from the monitor and keyboard. The most successful arrangement seemed to be to have the monitor above and the keyboard and disc drive on a trapezium shaped table with the narrow end as the three sides that the children sat around. With the rectangular table the children tended to move together to form a threesome leaving one child isolated at the end of the table. The trapezium brought the group physically closer together and seemed the best arrangement to encourage collaborative talk. Initially half hour sessions were allocated to children for work with the computer but this proved impractical since motivation was often high and it would have been short sighted to disturb such concentrated effort. It seemed appropriate then that sessions should vary in length depending on the nature of the work and the overall organisation of the school day. Sessions varied in length lasting up to one hour.

When examining the teacher's role and comparing what was said and done by the two groups A and B the following organisational points seemed to be important:

(a) Groups of all abilities can work around the microcomputer depending on the reading level demanded by the program, but mixed ability grouping seemed to take care of potential reading problems since the better readers read to the poorer readers.

(b) There is a need for back up material which will minimise the need for teacher intervention in certain areas. In this case whole class teaching, the *Granny's Garden* wordbank and training in handling discs and computers fostered independence from the start and minimised unnecessary organisational demands on the teacher.

(c) It is necessary for the teacher to know programs well, to have clearly defined aims for their use and to arrange groups and group work accordingly.

(d) Teacher time with a group working at the computer can be best spent by slowing children down and asking questions that promote reasoning, logical thinking and prediction.

The observed groups worked on *Granny's Garden* in sessions that totalled seven hours. Throughout this time there was constant talk. Talk was not confined to the microcomputer alone. Related discussion continued at playtime and at home. Talk around the computer was almost wholly on task even in sessions up to one hour long. Even in the off task comments it was possible to find some links with the computer, e.g. James (to Louise): "You've got trees in your eyes 'cos it reflects into your glasses". (referring to the 12 magic trees on the screen).

One could ascribe the high level of concentration to the fact that the whole exercise was a novel experience but it continued for the duration of the investigation.

Tables 1 and 2 show the total number of utterances by the two groups during three sessions on the computer.

Table 1: The distribution of talk in Group A.

Name	Utterances per session			
	1	2	3	Total
Andrea	67	31	213	321
Louise	43	25	115	183
Thomas	35	16	66	117
James	32	8	60	100

Table 2: The distribution of talk in Group B.

Name	Utterances per session			
	1	2	3	Total
Michelle	157	44	141	342
Angela	170	42	124	336
Adam	64	58	153	275
Tom	109	15	60	184

The total number of utterances by all children shows a willingness by all members of the group to contribute. The high number of utterances by Andrea can be explained by her tendency to organise the group and to do much of the reading from the screen. James's small number of contributions might be explained by the fact that he had a poorer reading ability than the other members of the group.

The analysis of the talk generated while using the computer was undertaken using Tough's Model for Appraisal (1981). From the tape recordings taken and transcribed two were selected as examples one from each of the groups A and B when they were working on "The Woodcutter's Cottage" section of the program. Each utterance by the children was considered and placed in the appropriate category (see Tables 3 and 4).

Tough (1981) expands on each of these categories. She writes that the ability to report on past experiences, to reason logically, to anticipate and predict the

Table 3: Language use in Group A.

Talk type	Number of utterances
Self-maintaining	29
Directing	40
Reporting	25
Towards logical reasoning	23
Predicting	26
Projecting	2
Imagining	2

Table 4: Language use in Group B.

Talk type	Number of utterances
Self-maintaining	35
Directing	79
Reporting	60
Towards logical reasoning	36
Predicting	13
Projecting	8
Imagining	0

outcome of events, to survey possibilities of alternative courses of action, to recognise problems and reflect on their solution and to project into the lives and feelings of others and into situations which they have not experienced is crucial for learning. One might conclude, therefore, that "quality" talk is when children demonstrate their verbal ability to draw on past experiences, think logically and solve problems. Some reference to the children's talk as found in these two transcripts and their relationship to the categories outlined by Tough (1981) follows.

The use of self-maintaining language was fairly evenly spread throughout the session and between the groups. The language used demonstrated physical want, the protection of self interest, the justification of behaviour and criticism of others. Much of the self-maintaining language was concerned with the practical issues of whose turn it was to operate the keyboard and read the monitor. When there is sharing, co-operation and turn taking it is likely that there will be evidence of self-maintaining language.

Using language in order to direct was particularly high, especially in group B where the teacher was not fully involved and so the group had to take on the role of directing themselves and others. This seems to indicate that children are able to organise themselves independently when they are interested and know what they want to achieve.

The transcripts show that the reporting by the children is not particularly complex. It included labelling, referring to detail and incidents. For much of the time the reporting was fairly obvious and brief. There is more language used for logical reasoning by group B, the children working without direct teacher help, than by group A. It might, therefore, be the case that the teacher's questions were not important in encouraging the use of logical reasoning and that the nature of the activity was sufficient to promote this kind of language. However, where instances of logical reasoning do appear in the group B transcript they have often been preceded by a question asked by the teacher.

The use of language for prediction offers interesting results. For although there were less utterances overall in group A than group B, group A used language to predict twice as often as group B. Almost every example of prediction given by a group A child follows a question or comment from the teacher. Such examples of prediction from group A are more specific and detailed than those found in the group B discussions.

Both projecting and imagining play a small part in the discussions as Tables 3 and 4 show. It is possible that without specific teacher help the program was not conducive to promoting language of this nature with children of this age and ability.

If the teacher is aware that self-maintaining, directing and reporting will probably accompany most work on the computer then she can focus specifically on encouraging logical reasoning, prediction, projection and imagining. She may also feel that it is useful for her to spend time on extending the type and quality of reporting. It would seem that teacher intervention may also make an effective contribution to the children's learning and discussion by ensuring that the contribution of the quieter members of the group is not lost.

In spite of the brief time spent on this investigation the general implications and findings would seem to have application to most classroom settings. In these three weeks almost every child in the class became a competent keyboard operator and independent microcomputer user. All the groups were given the opportunity to develop their ability to think logically, their problem solving skills, their reading, spelling and note-making abilities and their social skills in interacting and co-operating with the rest of the group. The children were involved in both reading and writing for a purpose. One would hope that during the course of the project the skills and abilities described above were extended. It did seem that the computer promoted and encouraged on task and independent discussion which showed evidence of approved language strategies, something not always possible with other group activities in the classroom particularly without continued teacher intervention.

Having completed this investigation we have begun to appreciate and recognise the potential which working with the microcomputer holds for the non-expert and have discovered that 'used well, the microcomputer could provide a powerful tool in the development of language skills'. (Futcher, 1984).

References

Bleach, P. (1984) Chips Champion. *Times Educational Supplement*, 29.6.84, 41.

Fox, D. (1986) Talking and Learning with Microcomputers. *Education 3-13*, 29-33

Fox, P. (1985) Some aspects of Language Development in the Infant School and the opportunities which arise for Computer based Activities. In *Infants and First Schools: the Role of the Microcomputer*. Council for Educational Technology.

Futcher, D. (1984) Developing Reading and Language Skills. *Educational Computing*, 27-33.

MEP (1984) *Language Development in the Primary School: the Role of the Microcomputer*. Council for Educational Technology.

MEP (1985) *Infants and First Schools: The Role of the Microcomputer*. Council for Educational Technology.

Potter, F.N. (1985) *Classroom Organisation and Group Discussion: the role of the Microcomputer, the role of the Teacher*. Edge Hill College of Higher Education.

Robinson, B. (1985) *Microcomputers and the Language Arts*. Milton Keynes: Open University Press.

Schenk, C. (1984a) Language Extensions. *Times Educational Supplement*, 2.3.84, 40.

Schenk, C. (1984b) Talking Point. In *Language Development in the Primary School, The Role of the Microcomputer*. Council for Educational Technology.

Tough, J. (1981) *Listening to Children Talking*. London: Ward Lock Educational.

Using a TTNS Electronic Mailbox in a Junior Class : A Case Study

Elizabeth Wishart

The TTNS Electronic Mailbox

The Times Network Systems, or TTNS for short, uses a channel of Telecom Gold. It was established in 1985 as a means whereby schools and other educational institutions might communicate with each other through an electronic mailbox and access certain national and regional databases quickly and easily at a subsidised rate. This account is only concerned with the use of the electronic mailbox. This is operated by connecting the microcomputer to the telephone line via a "black box" or modem. Messages are sent and received in a matter of seconds by using the software supplied by TTNS on payment of an annual subscription which depends upon the size of the school. A further payment provides an international link through Telecom Gold to schools in many other countries, as far afield as Australia and New Zealand.

Telephone charges are extra but not excessive, since it is possible to use local telephone line for all calls and the costs can be further reduced by preparing outgoing mail on disc. In this form messages can be sent more quickly and therefore more cheaply than by typing messages live into the computer, which uses more on line time. Incoming mail can be printed out for reading easily and at the most convenient time of day.

Some LEAs have taken subscriptions for a large number of their schools and in other authorities individual schools have joined as independent members. Where membership is widespread in an authority, projects and collaborative activities are often coordinated by a system manager who has had training in the use of the network and who operates the central LEA mailbox. This person may be a teacher with computer expertise who offers guidance to schools. In the absence of LEA membership, individual schools can work independently within the system by making contact with other schools through the directory and establishing their own initiatives. All member schools can use the international network and build projects based on the links through this.

The school featured in this case study was a small rural primary school of eighty four children which took out its own subscription to TTNS independently of the authority which did not activate its central mail box until more than a year later. The use of the link by the "top" class was observed week by week in a non-participatory way over two academic years. In the first year of the study the class was a small, one age class of fourth years who were starting their second year in the "top" class and who had had some exposure to TTNS as members of a mixed age class of third and fourth years in the preceding year. In the second year of the study the new "top" class was a mixed age class of third and four years who were less experienced than their predecessors at wordprocessing and who had had little exposure to TTNS.

The reasons for introducing electronic mail

Three factors informed the decision to introduce an electronic mail link to the classroom. Firstly there was concern about the place of technology in the curriculum. Secondly contexts were being sought for language development which would provide real opportunities for the pupils to write for different purposes and audiences and practice oral language skills. Thirdly ways were being examined in which links with other schools might be developed and extended.

The school had had a microcomputer since the Department of Industry made them available to all primary schools in 1982. To begin with, the focus was on using the technology rather than understanding how the computer could be made to work for the user. The way in which much of the software demanded a reactive rather than an active role in learning was not deemed to be supportive to the school's existing curriculum, and ways were sought to modernise the curriculum technologically while retaining the important features which allowed the pupils to exercise their initiative and to be in control of the technology. Additions were made to the existing hardware, through the purchase of word processing facilities, disc drives and a printer. The arrival of TTNS in 1985 appeared to offer the means to extend and develop the use of these and to broaden the pupils curriculum encounters. The real data gathered from live sources via the mailbox could complement work in mathematics, history, geography, science and the language arts.

The Bullock report (1975) had recommended that children should have genuine purposes and audiences for writing and that they should progressively be able to recognise and adopt different writing styles. In the Kingman report (1988) these recommendations were reiterated. The electronic mailbox appeared to offer experience in just these ways and the decision to introduce it appeared to be a valuable extension to existing classroom practice.

Direct links with other schools through the mailbox might also have the potential to provide a peer group challenge in particular, for the more able pupils. For example a school situated in a locality of special interest historically or industrially might build up resources about the locality for others to use. An electronic link could facilitate cooperation, too, between staff, for example, a teacher with expertise in Science might set up a collaborative programme between several schools. Attention was drawn to this kind of possibility by Professor Ted Wragg in his address to the National Association in Support of Small Schools at their annual conference in 1987, when he discussed the benefits which might accrue to small schools through electronic links, in terms of exchanging ideas and information and sharing the learning potential of interesting projects.

Since on examination, a TTNS mailbox seemed to have the potential to meet the desired objectives, a modem was purchased and the decision was taken to join the network.

How electronic mail was used

The case study school was a small one of eighty four pupils in four classes. All through the school the children worked independently with some measure of choice and they were familiar with the computer from the reception class where programmes such as Podd were in regular use.

The informal atmosphere which prevailed in this small community gave rise to a lot of incidental sharing between children and all classes knew something of what each other was doing. The top juniors used their wordprocessing skills to write their own multi-ended stories. Also they have worked with other local schools in the past on serial story writing. For this they have had to send their discs by post because the schools with whom they worked had no TTNS mailbox.

The two classes observed in the two consecutive years were different in composition and experience of the technology and so there were substantial differences in what was observed from year to year. The fourth year class, observed in the first year of the class study had obtained some knowledge of TTNS during their third year which they had spent in the "top" class with the same teacher. They took responsibility for the practical operation of the mailbox, sharing their expertise with each other and using the terminology and procedures easily. This was evident from their conversations with each other in the classroom. The tasks relating to the orderly use of the network, for example keeping a record of mail sent, received and answered, were recognised and carried out. The mail was usually printed first thing in the morning and responsibilities and priorities were discussed and allocated then and carried out at an appropriate time. Sometimes messages were relayed during the course of a lesson, if this was necessary, but generally messages were prepared by pupils during the day, on their individual discs and sent towards the end of the day's work. This is not only simpler but more economical.

In the first year of the observation the children started by exchanging information daily about the weather with a school in the Shetland Islands. Two boys took responsibility for collecting, sending and receiving this data. Graphs were made of the local weather information and that from the Shetlands and these were compared and discussed in the classroom.

Letters were also exchanged between the children and the content of those received provided starting points for a study of the islanders, their lifestyle, language and traditions, the fishing industry and oil refining as well as the wildlife of the islands. The children found this live contact very motivating, their interest was sustained over a long period as they worked from resources provided in the classroom. It was also the case that they learned about their own environment purposefully and sought to present this information interestingly and accurately in order to send it to their correspondents. The work to which the TTNS link gave rise required them to use the basic skills, some of which they learnt in formal sessions and some of which they had to acquire for the purposes of the project, as well as their talents in expressive arts and science. The project culminated in a comprehensive display for the school and parents. Later TTNS created a national database for weather information to which the class continued to contribute for the rest of that school year. This helped them to learn the need for systematic data collection when scientific comparisons are to be made. However the motivation was not as strong as it was when the human element was present and this activity was not continued in the second year with the new "top" class.

During the year a number of different projects were initiated, some of which complemented work in hand, others developed from contacts made and some were initiated by individuals for their own interest. A study of the variations in the cost of living across the country, made by gathering data at intervals, of the cost of a 'shopping basket' complemented work in mathematics. A mini-project on Bonnie Prince Charlie arose from a contact with a school not too far from the site of the battle of Culloden. One girl, an able flute player, initiated her own survey of musical instruments played in primary schools. Data from an exchange of information about fathers' occupations in different areas of the country gave rise to a discussion of unemployment, something which the pupils did not know from their own experience and which they found difficult to comprehend.

The children participated in a range of different kinds of projects from other schools too, for example a survey of playground games, which required them to give descriptions. Information about the school and the environment was sought by other schools for varying purposes and the children learnt to deal with such requests economically and to make full use of their research.

A popular activity which took place termly was the centrally organised newspaper day. For this the school hall was set up with a 'desk' responsible for each main news section, national news, international news, sport, fashion and local news. All the junior children joined in this activity and sometimes they invited children from another school. The network transmitted the news from a central point, this was passed to the appropriate 'desk' where children selected and prepared items for the compositors, at work next door. A separate team collected local news and interviews for inclusion. Several different computer programs were used to prepare headlines and format pages and when the paper was ready, copies were prepared for sale. TTNS was the main single news source, however the variety of work involved in making the newspaper allowed all the children to participate in some way. Children used different skills and talents and there had to be a high degree of cooperation to meet the deadline for photocopying and collating at the end of the school day. Lower junior children gained some experience of TTNS through participating in this activity.

In April, some months after the start of the study, the LEA made TTNS available to six additional schools with a view to running a collaborative project based on an agricultural college and culminating in a display of work on farming at the end of the summer term. These schools were new to TTNS and some were situated too far from the college to arrange a visit conveniently. The time was very short and therefore only limited collaboration between schools was achieved. However in the case study school, data on milk yields were collected from the college and this provided a real context for mathematics. The TTNS link was the starting point for a programme of visits and investigations related to the project which the children found very motivating and which produced work in history, geography and science. Since the case study school was accomplished in the use of TTNS it helped the other schools to get started and two of these schools used the international link to find out about farming in Australia. These schools are still working with their overseas links one year later.

The class observed in the second year of the study was a mixed age group one of third and fourth year children. They began the year with little exposure to TTNS and with rather fewer wordprocessing skills than their predecessors. The class was larger in numbers and included a less mature group of young children. It was necessary to make haste slowly. In the first term they developed their wordprocessing skills in the course of producing a fortnightly school newspaper, for sale. They also became fluent with other software but they did not use the electronic mailbox. In the second term they joined in the TTNS newspaper and selected children went to the TTNS centre to help in transmitting news to participating schools. The children were successful with these activities and they enjoyed themselves but it was the only activity in their curriculum which involved the electronic mailbox. This limitation was a deliberate decision taken by the teacher who thought it important to develop the pupils' skills and competence to manage the mailbox themselves before introducing it. The benefits of this will probably be seen in next year's fourth year group.

Some advantages and problems of using a TTNS mailbox

The decision to introduce the mailbox and to create the opportunity for live contact with other schools and institutions afforded some clear advantages to the fourth year group of children observed in the first year of the study. They were highly motivated and capable with the procedures and their use of language improved more than the teacher had expected. The children recognised spontaneously when something from another school appeared to have been written by a teacher and they grew critical of expression and careful of their presentation when they were sending material to other schools. Understandably, perhaps, they did not always apply the same standards to their preparatory research in the classroom. There were personal and social benefits too. The pupils gained in confidence in pursuing their own ideas. They learned to be explicit and make their meaning clear when sending their messages and requests. Along with this they learned the implications for themselves of asking for someone else's collaboration and they experienced other people's perceptions and examined other points of view. They also learned the discipline of dealing regularly and systematically with the mail box in order not to get in a muddle. They liked the immediacy and the live encounters which the direct links offered.

The potential of TTNS forecast when the TES reported its establishment in 1985 - that it would develop confidence in expression, fluency with the technology, and that the children would learn to understand their work in the on text of the world of work and gain knowledge of other people's lifestyles across the country - was supported by these children's responses to questions about TTNS. They could explain what it was and what it could do and they thought that it was fun and that the projects to which it gave rise were interesting. They preferred writing with the wordprocessor to using a pen. The most important benefits of TTNS for them, were that it was fast and that the information obtained through the mailbox was up to date. None of them questioned its accuracy or expressed the need to compare one source with another. Perhaps this reflected their trust in their teacher not to allow them to be misled.

These gains from TTNS were offset by some difficulties. In the year that the observations were started there was a great deal of diverse activity arising from TTNS and it was very hard work for the teachers to weld it all into a coherent pattern and ensure that all the necessary resources were available to support the work away from the computer so as to do justice to a topic and bring it to completion. For this reason, as well as because of the different level of skill and competence of the children the decision was taken to limit the use of the mailbox in the second year. Although the use which was made of the mailbox in the second year was successful in terms of the objectives set, namely to provide experience with technology as a means in the control of the user to extend language experience and to provide direct links outside the school, nevertheless the cost must become an important factor if there is such limited use.

From time to time problems were encountered with the operation of the technology. While it is quite easy to learn the routines for sending and receiving mail, the technology does not always respond as expected. Small problems can waste time and they can be very frustrating for children. The handbook is not comprehensive or easily intelligible to the uninitiated, the system is not user friendly, in that the help which there is within it is hard to find. These points are of considerable importance where there is just one enthusiastic and knowledgeable teacher in a school. If that teacher is absent and no one else can oversee the work, then valuable time is lost at both ends of a link. Indeed, if the one knowledgeable person leaves the school, the use of the mailbox may cease.

Conclusion

Some suggestions can be offered about the conditions which appear to be necessary before the potential of the electronic mailbox can be exploited fully. First, the pupils need to have attained a certain degree of competence with wordprocessing and to be able to write intelligibly and independently. Secondly, their teacher needs a flexible teaching style in order to meet the demands which arise. In a school which takes a view of the curriculum commensurate with a strongly transmission oriented approach to teaching, it may be difficult to integrate the activities to which direct links with other schools give rise. Thirdly, where local leadership or locally coordinated projects are not available, prior contact between teachers in, say, two or three schools which might work together could usefully be sought, in order to ensure a focus and commitment to see a project through and to facilitate the provision of appropriate resources. If a link with a school in the southern hemisphere is developed, it is important to remember that the school year ends in December and not in July, so that plans for continuity can be made. Fourthly, it is important that there should be more than one teacher in a school, even a small one, who is competent in the use of the system to ensure continuity and make the expenditure on the equipment and the subscription worthwhile, particularly while information about the system remains somewhat inaccessible. Lastly, a separate telephone line is generally a luxury and so it is important to arrange with the secretary for convenient times to use the school line.

For upper junior children with some wordprocessing and writing skill, the electronic mailbox has been shown to offer a purposeful experience of technology and many varied contexts for using language in different ways have been demonstrated along with some of the special benefits of direct links and live contacts with other schools. However perhaps the most important factors in its successful use for the benefit of children, are the degree of commitment and enthusiasm of the teacher, both to find the financial support and to maintain the necessary level of resources in the classroom.

References

DES (1975) *A Language for Life*, HMSO

DES (1988) *The Teaching of English*. London. HMSO

Wragg, E. (1987) Address to the National Association for the Support of Small Schools (Unpublished)

Reading Screens: Mapping the Labyrinth

Vivienne Cato, Fiona English and John Trushell

The rate at which the microcomputer is being adopted as a versatile classroom resource for language activities threatens to outstrip understanding of how pupils perceive and use it.

Pupils can engage in purposeful discussion while conducting an adventure game/ simulation, interrogating a database or word processing a composition. Both collaborative and individual work on a word processor can help pupils acquire an understanding of writing processes while 'effortlessly' re-drafting their 'product'. However, the use of these programs presumes the pupils' ability to read instructions or information on-screen.

Introduction

Unlike print the microcomputer can potentially help the reader interrogate text by providing reading access to mediating options. Joan Feeley (1985) looks forward to the future when programs may provide 'dynamic books': these, according to L.E. and O.P. Geoffrion (1985), would be:

a multidimensional learning environment where the reader can browse through the material according to personal goals and needs. The computer masks the intrusiveness of searching for material, by locating and displaying different portions automatically.

A prototype program, devised by Reinking and Schreiner (1985), provided the reader with a range of mediating options that are not easily accessible to readers of traditional text: further background, main paragraph ideas, easier version and vocabulary.

These mediations were based on advice from experienced teachers. Fifty-two strong and fifty-two weak readers (11-12 year olds) were randomly selected to participate in the study. Readers were randomly assigned to four different presentations of three high and three low difficulty texts. The four experimental groups were offered the following:

1. *Off line* - text in-print with no textual manipulations,
2. *Text Only* - text on-screen with no textual manipulations,
3. *Select Options* - text on-screen provided with manipulations, from which pupils were free to choose and

4. *All Options* - text on-screen provided with manipulations which all pupils were obliged to view.

Notably the study did not include a group of pupils using text in-print provided with resources equivalent to those offered to the on-screen group.

The options most frequently chosen by pupils in the Select Options group was further background. The option least frequently chosen by good readers was vocabulary but by poor readers was main paragraph idea. Pupils seldom chose to re-read the texts.

Pupils performed better on low difficulty tests when reading from print rather than on-screen except the All Options group who produced similar or marginally better performances. However, pupils in the All Options group reading high difficulty texts, whether strong or weak readers, performed significantly better than their Off-Line counterparts.

Further research concerned with the effects of text on-screen on reader performance was undertaken by Gambrell et al. (1987) who conducted a study with 8 and 10 year olds. The researchers selected two reading texts considered to be within the capabilities of 8 year olds and 10 year olds respectively. Each text was presented both in-print and on-screen to pupils of the appropriate ages. The participating pupils, randomly allocated to read either text in-print or text on-screen, had all had some microcomputer experience.

Those pupils reading texts from screen were able to initiate requests for new pages by pressing a key. The readers of print were free to use the booklet however they wished. The pupils were expected to complete three written tasks: 'free recall' in the form of retelling to a friend, 'cued recall' of 8 items, and attitude responses to 6 items.

Results showed that there was no statistically significant difference in performance when reading texts on-screen as opposed to text in-print. However, older pupils tended to perform slightly better on 'free recall' and 'cued recall' tasks on-screen rather than in-print, whereas the opposite was true for the younger group.

Both groups expressed the opinion that text in-print was easier to read and understand, although there was a tendency for pupils to rate text on-screen higher in terms of enjoyment.

These studies reported in this study presented primary pupils with text on-screen co-ordinated by an index - a simple manipulation - within a program. The readers' strategies, while locating within the program specific information required to complete a variety of tasks, were observed and the pupils' individual performances in-print and on-screen were compared.

Organisation

The study was conducted by researchers with the co-operation of teachers in a middle school in Slough. The school had access to two BBC micro-computers which were provided with 40 track disc-drives. This equipment was supplemented by a further micro-computer and three 80 track disc-drives provided by the NFER. The pupils had not previously had substantial experience with microcomputers, and particularly not in reading and manipulating screens of text.

The reading materials for the study, "Sweet Success" and "Comic Story", had been devised as tests for the Assessment of Performance Unit (APU). Each test in-print had been administered to a sample of three hundred and fifty pupils (approximately) during the Primary Pilot Survey, Summer Term 1987. These tests were subsequently adapted for presentation on-screen.

This study was conducted in two phases during one week in the Summer Term 1988. Thirty six third year pupils (10-11 year olds) were chosen to participate in the study. The pupils were arranged in two randomly-chosen but equivalent sub-samples, A and B. The pupils of sub-sample A were presented with 'Sweet Success' in-print to be completed individually, then presented with 'Comic Story' on-screen to be completed collaboratively in groups of three. The collaborative groups were formed on the basis of alphabetical ordering of surnames. The pupils of sub-sample B were presented with 'Comic Story' in-print, then 'Sweet Success' on-screen, both of which were to be completed individually. All tests were presented as untimed, but in practice both in-print and on-screen versions took approximately one hour.

The date collected from the study were:

1. observations of the strategies the pupils employed in reading text on-screen and completing the written answers, and
2. two completed answer booklets from each pupil (total 72)

The data concerning individual pupil performance on the tests enabled comparisons to be made:

1. between the performances on the tests by the APU Pilot Study sample and the two sub-samples of this study, in-print, and
2. between performances on 'Sweet Success' in-print and on-screen.

Description of Materials and Tasks

Materials

The APU Pilot Survey reading materials 'Sweet Success' and 'Comic Story' were printed on A4 pages (70 characters to a line, 40 lines to a page) and bound as booklets ('Sweet Success' comprised 5 pages; 'Comic Story' comprised 6 pages). The complementary answer booklets were a similar format.

These reading materials were adapted for display in screen-windows (56 characters to a line, 29 lines to a screen-window) co-ordinated by an index into programs ('Sweet Success' comprised 9 screen-windows; 'Comic Story' comprised 11 screen windows). The programs were structured so that readers could gain access from the index to any screen, access from screen to screen sequentially and access from any screen to the index.

Both in-print and on-screen, texts were both presented in block paragraphs, or 'chunked'. Text which was italicised for emphasis in-print was highlighted for emphasis on-screen. Although text in-print was double-spaced, text on-screen was single-spaced due to constructions of space within-screen-windows.

Pupils' readings of texts on-screen and in-print were all tested with a selection of exercises printed in answer booklets identical to those of the APU Pilot Survey.

Tasks

For the purposes of this study, five tasks were selected from the answer booklet which complemented the text 'Sweet Success'. Each task required pupils to select information and reformulate it within a given format. The tasks are described here in what proved to be ascending order of difficulty for pupils whether participating in the APU Pilot Survey or in this study. The number in brackets refers to their order of appearance in the answer booklet.

Task A: Illustrated Description to Labelled Illustration (1): Screen 1 contained a short passage describing the features of the cacao tree, accompanied by an illustration (Extract 1). Implicit in the description were details which had to be selected to label that illustration replicated in the answer book.

Task B: Table to Bar Chart Completion (5): Screen 7 featured a three-column table listing, in alphabetical order, twenty brands of confectionery and the quantity of sugar each contained (adapted from Tudge, 1985). The answer booklet provided a bar chart that re-listed these brands in order of increasing quantity of sugar.

Omitted from the bar chart were selected brands which pupils were required to identify and label (Example 1). Despite the change in format, the source of the necessary information was once more readily apparent to the pupils. Although each presentation featured a listing of products, not all pupils perceived the differing principles of order underlying them.

Task C: Xocoatl: Prose to Cloze (3): Screen 3 contained a passage describing the making of an Aztec cocoa drink, Xocoatl. The ingredients embedded in this passage had to be identified to complete a recipe for Xocoatl: a list of the ingredients had to be compiled, then the ingredients had to be inserted appropriately into an incomplete set of instructions.

Task D: Morning Cocoa: Prose to Statement Organisation (2): Screens 3 and 3 featured passages which provided an account of the history of drinking chocolate: from these passages, information had to be selected and organised to complete a recipe for Morning Cocoa. Organisation took the form of correctly numbering jumbled instructions (see Example 2).

Task E: Chocolate Making: Prose to Table Completion (4): Screen 3 contained a passage from which information had to be selected to complete a table summarising key points in the history of chocolate making (see Example 3). All columns of the last row are blank, making it impossible to locate information by matching names or dates.

Sweet Success: on-screen presented pupils with an additional task: to read and use the index which co-ordinated the screens (see Extract 3). Pupils may have inferred from the index - the co-ordination of numbered screens with different titles - the sequence and sum of screens to be read.

Extract 1

Cacao trees are evergreen trees which blossom twice yearly. White, yellow, pink or red, delicate blossoms sprout on the lower branches and trunk. Some of these blossoms develop into pods. These pods ripen within four to six months. The golden ripe pods are about fifteen to twenty five centimetres long. Inside the pods there are between twenty to forty cocoa beans.

Example 1

Sugar Content of Selected Chocolates

Example 2

The instructions for the Morning Cocoa recipe are in the wrong order - please number the instructions, in order, from 1 to 5.

Morning Cocoa

Ingredients	*Utensils*	*Instructions*
Dried cocoa beans	A pan	* Stir cakes into hot water.
Cinnamon	A spoon	* Heat water in a pan until boiling.
Vanilla	A grinder	* Leave paste to cool and harden into small cakes.
Water Sugar	A cup per person	
Cream		* Serve with cream and sweeten with sugar to taste.
		* Grind dried cocoa beans into a paste with vanilla cinnamon.

Extract 2

(Screen 2) The Spanish blended the cocoa paste with vanilla and cinnamon. The Spanish cocoa drink was served hot and sweetened with sugar. The preparation of cocoa remained a Spanish secret for almost a hundred years.

(Screen 3) In 1660, when the French King married a Spanish princess, cocoa was taken to France. The French preferred cocoa sweetened with sugar and served with cream.

Eventually, a Frenchman opened a shop in London which sold cakes of cocoa from which to make the drink. Cocoa was scarce and very expensive, but the drinking of cocoa became fashionable with the wealthy. Ladies drank cocoa for their breakfast. Gentleman chose to drink cocoa in their coffee-houses.

Example 3

INDEX

Screen 1: Cacao-trees
Screen 2: Aztecs. Spaniards and Xocoatl
Screen 3: Cocoa and Chocolate
Screen 4: Growing Cacao-trees
Screen 5: World Regional Cocoa Production
Screen 6: Rare Cocoa to Commonplace Chocolate

Screen 7: Sugar Content of Selected Chocolates
Screen 8: Recipe - Ingredients and Utensils
Screen 9: Recipe - Instructions
To read a screen, press screen number (1-9)

Pupils' Performance of Tasks

In this study, pupils' individual performance on both tests in-print conformed with the performance of the sample of the APU Pilot Survey. However, pupils' individual performance on 'Sweet Success' on-screen was at variance with the performance of the APU Pilot Survey.

Pupils were more successful at completing certain exercises when information had been selected from text on-screen rather than in-print; labelling the illustration of a cacao-tree (Task A) and completing the bar chart (Task B). Whether selecting information from text on-screen or in-print, pupils were equally successful at completing the cloze procedure section of the Xocoatl recipe (Task C) and organizing instructions for the Morning Cocoa recipe (Task D). Pupils were less successful at completing the remaining exercises when information was on-screen: that is, listing the ingredients for and defining the meaning of Xocoatl (Task C) and completing the table on chocolate making (Task E).

Tasks A and B

The formats for Tasks A and B have antecedents in the text, whether in-print or on-screen: Task A reproduces the illustration of a cacao-tree; Task B reprises the list of confectionery brands. The information required to provide the content to complete Tasks A and B coincides in the text with these antecedents (page 1 and 4 in booklet; screens 1 and 7 in program).

However, within the program, the index indicates the location of both illustration and table (Screen 1: Cacao-trees, and Screen 7: Sugar Content of Selected Chocolates). Moreover, Task A and B have a greater emphasis on-screen than in-print. The illustration for Task A occupies a half of Screen 1 but only a quarter of a page 1; the description, coincident with the illustration which provides the information for Task A, occupies a half of Screen 1 but a quarter of page 1. The table, which provides the information for Task B, occupies all of Screen 7 but a half of page 4. Thus, the success of pupils performing these tasks from texts on-screen may be attributed to the greater discernibility of the required information within the program and within a screen.

Tasks C and D

The format for Tasks C and D has a precedent in the text, in-print or on-screen: both tasks are in a recipe format derived from an example in the text for 'Chocolate Chinchilla' (adapted from David, 1970). However, the information required to complete Tasks C and D does not coincide with the example recipe (page 5 in booklet; screens 8 and 9 in program) but in passages of prose (pages 1 and 2 in booklet; screens 2 and 3 in program).

Pupils reading text on-screen were clearly observed to return to those screens which featured the recipe (Screen 8: Recipe - Ingredients and Utensils, and Screen 9: Recipe - Instructions). Although the location of the information required for Task C was indicated at the index (Screen 2: Aztecs, Spaniards and Xocoatl) pupils were observed frequently to locate this information by the highlighted term xocoatl while 'skimming' screens. The information required by Task D was also located while 'skimming', although it could have been selected from the index (Screen 3: Cocoa and Chocolate, or Screen 6: Rare Cocoa to Commonplace Chocolate). Pupils performing these tasks from texts on-screen did not locate the required information by reading the index but frequently attempted to discern the information from either the format ('Chocolate Chinchilla') or features (highlighted xocoatl) of passages with screens.

Task E

The tabular format for Task E has no antecedent in the text. The information for that task is contained in a passage of prose (page 2 in booklet; screen 3 in program). Although the information required for this task could have been selected from the index (Screen 3: Cocoa and Chocolate, or Screen 6: Rare Cocoa to Commonplace Chocolate) the location was not greatly discernible by 'skimming' screens. Pupils reading text on-screen found the information with difficulty: in fact, Task E was more frequently omitted by pupils reading text on-screen than in-print (4:1).

The Index

Observations of pupils' performance would indicate that, although screens were accessed from the index, they were seldom selected by their pertinence to the various tasks. Pupils were frequently observed to locate information relevant to particular tasks by rapidly 'skimming' screens, either individually or sequentially, for discernible format or features of passages.

Pupils re-read the text extensively: screen selections per pupil averaged 57, and ranged between 12 and 103, in an hour (approximately).

However, few pupils were observed to have inferred, from the index, either the complement of screens, or the sequence in which those screens should be read. The complement of nine screens had not been accessed by:

1. two thirds of the pupils within ten selections,
2. half of the pupils within twenty selections and
3. a quarter of the pupils within thirty selections.

Two pupils never accessed the complement of nine screens. Moreover, a third of pupils' first selection from the index was a screen other than Screen 1.

Those few pupils whose first selection from the index was Screen 1 and who then accessed the complement of screens sequentially generally performed better: in fact, the performance of these pupils on 'Sweet Success' on-screen equalled or excelled their performance on 'Comic Story' in-print. The factor common to these pupils, who comprised a quarter of the sample, was the strategies they employed, not their ability.

Summary

The performance of pupils in this study reading text in-print conforms with the performance of a nationally representative sample. A comparison of performance in-print and on-screen discloses that pupils generally perform less well locating information on-screen than in-print: in particular, pupils were least successful at locating information within prose passages on-screen.

The provision of the index to co-ordinate the screens of text disclosed that a large proportion of pupils did not infer the principle or purpose of an index. However, the performance of those pupils who accessed the text sequentially from the index equalled or excelled their performance in-print on the companion test.

Discussion

Primary pupils' use of an index has featured in the surveys of the APU, which found that:

low scorers were able to pick out relevant items or topics using an index or contents page with near to fifty per cent accuracy, while high performers frequently did this with complete accuracy. (Gorman and Kispal, 1987)

However, these indices occurred in-print. Due to the conventionality and the corporeity of text in-print, a structure may be attributed which an index only elaborates. Unconventional and incorporeal text presented on-screen has an implicit structure which indices, or 'menus', make explicit.

Haas and Hayes (1986) have reported that adults experience problems in locating information in word processed text. They demonstrated that locating, retrieving and comprehending textual information displayed on-screens was more difficult than reading from print-out.

The structure and location of information within texts in-print are memorised only incidentally to reading. However, the structure and location of information must be committed to memory concurrently with reading text on-screen, otherwise readers may become disorientated within the program.

Corporeity was a criterion when pupils participating in this study expressed a preference for texts in-print or on-screen:

Using the micro is harder ... because you can't find what you want easily ... because you have to press keys, you can't flick over.

It takes a bit longer on the computer ... in the book you can flick back easily and find out.

Although in this study pupils were generally inaccurate when using the index of the program "Sweet Success", there is evidence from studies involving mathematics programs (Holmes et al., 1985; Robson et al., 1988) that pupils' strategies develop with experience.

For most individuals there was a tendency to make more varied choices as experience was gained. This is perhaps evidence of the development of a repertoire of strategies rather than the monopoly of just one. (Robson et al., 1988)

Readers, with experience, will become accustomed to the conventions of the microcomputer medium, the genres of program - e.g. data-bases, e-mail and simulations - and the structure of various texts and documents.

Nevertheless, each microcomputer program should include an explicit representation of the structure underlying and co-ordinating its text on-screen.

References

David, E. (1970) *Spices, salt and aromatics in the English kitchen.* London: Penguin

Feeley, J. (1985) "The computer as a resource for teaching reading now and tomorrow" in B.Root (ed) *Resources for Reading: Proceedings of the 22nd Annual Conference of the UKRA.* London: Macmillan.

Gambrell, L.B., Bradley, V.N & McLaughline, E.M. (1987) Young children's comprehension and recall of computer screen displayed text. *Journal of Research in Reading,* 10(2): Sept.

Geoffrion, L.D. & Geoffrion, O.P. (1985) *Beyond the electronic workbook.* Paper presented at the International Reading Association, New Orleans.

Gorman, T. & Kispal, A. (1987) *The assessment of reading: pupils aged 11 and 15.* NFER - Nelson

Haas, C. & Hayes, J.R. (1986) What did I just say: reading problems in writing with the machine. *Research in the Teaching of English,* 20(1): Feb.

Holmes, N., Robson, E.G. & Steward, A.P. (1985) Learner control in computer-assisted learning. *Journal of Computer-Assisted Learning,* 1.

Reinking, D. & Schreiner, R. (1985) The effects of computer-mediated text on measures of reading comprehension & reading behaviour. *Reading Research Quarterly,* XX 5: Fall

Robson, E.G., Steward, A.P. & Whitfield, G.E. (1988) Pupils' learning choices in learning with computers. *Journal of Computer Assisted Learning,* 4.

Tudge, C. (1985) *The Food Connection.* London: BBC

Acknowledgements

The authors wish to express their gratitude to the teachers and pupils of St.Ethelbert's School, Slough, to the Department of Cybernetics, Reading University, and to their programmer, Julian Brooker.

Word processors creating a social context for learning

Kristiina Kumpulainen

Introduction

One of the most highly valued applications of computers in classrooms seems to be the use of word processors. They are seen as effective tools for the fostering of children's language development and as tools with production and revision capacities, are regarded as having a unique potential to support the aims of writing curricula with an emphasis on process (Dickinson, 1986; Campbell, 1988). The relative ease of modifying the text is seen as encouraging children to focus more on the meaning of their writing, and as making the transition from oral to written communication easier (Robinson, 1985). In addition, children using word processors as a part of their writing instruction appear to be stimulated to write as a process of exploration and discovery (Cochran-Smith, 1991). The use of word processors is also thought to accord well with views which regard writing and reading as the major ways in which children move to disembedded thinking (Hughes, 1990). Moreover, word processing with computers has been shown to be highly motivating for many children regardless of their ability, encouraging teachers and pupils to participate in collaborative activities (Dudley-Marling & Searle, 1989).

A closer look at studies of the use of word processing reveals that many of them have focussed on text production and ignored the social contexts made possible by word processing (Cochran-Smith, 1991). Little attention has been given to discovering how, and to what degree, the processes of composition are reflected in children's talk whilst undertaking collaborative tasks at the word processor. This is a serious gap since information about children's learning processes represented in talk may be as important as information about the quality of the actual product.

Despite the lack of research investigating children's language interactions whilst writing collaboratively at word processors, it appears that working in small groups as a form of teaching is commonly used with computers. The reasons for this are partly to do with the scarcity of computers in classrooms (Hall & Rhodes, 1986; Keith & Glover, 1987) but are also caused by a belief in the role of group discussion in the enhancement of learning (Barnes & Todd, 1977; Phillips, 1988). This belief is strongly based on theories which emphasize the social construction of knowledge (Vygotsky, 1978; Wertsch, 1991). Through small group discussions children with different levels of understanding are seen as constructing shared knowledge superior to their individual knowledge. In this sense children in small groups are characterized as working in their zone of proximal development.

Previous studies which have examined small group work at computers have indicated that group interaction is an extremely complex matter (Sutherland & Hoyles, 1987). Moreover, many factors have been found to have an effect on children's interactions in computer contexts and findings from studies concerned with social interaction at computers have been mixed. On one hand, computers have been found to encourage and promote discussion among children (Dickinson, 1986; King, 1989; Hooper, et al, 1989). Conflicting evidence, on the other hand, has indicated that the learning environment created by the use of computers is not that different from any other classroom learning contexts (Light, 1987; Peacock & Breese, 1990). It is as yet unclear, therefore, what 'different learning experiences' (Cochran-Smith, 1991) are facilitated by the collaborative use of word processors.

In order to investigate the nature of children's learning experiences as represented in talk one has to be able to interpret the use of oral language in relation to its social contexts. This implies understanding the meanings which particular social contexts and related uses of language have for the participants. As Hymes argues "the key to understanding language in context is to start, not with language, but with context" (Hymes, in Cazden, et al, 1972). In addition, when trying to study children's real capabilities in language it appears important to observe children in natural situations where they see the task as meaningful and feel ownership of it (Tizard & Hughes, 1984; Wells, 1987). The word processor may be able to create a learning environment that fulfils these requirements. It may lead children to use their language naturally and hence to reveal what they are really capable of achieving (Hughes, 1990). Analysis of this type of interaction appears to be worthy of investigation.

The present study

The study reported here aimed to investigate the nature of children's learning experiences in a word processing context by analysing the functions identified in children's talk during the process of collaborative writing at the computer. In addition, the study tried to gain a better understanding of the effects of group composition on children's language interactions at the word processor.

The study specifically addressed the following questions:

1) How would children use oral language during the process of collaborative writing at the word processor?

2) How would group composition affect children's language use and thinking processes at the word processor?

The work reported in this paper is part of a larger research project which was also designed to investigate the effects of attainment and gender on children's language use and thinking processes whilst working in small groups at the word processor. The findings related to these research questions will be discussed elsewhere.

The data collection was undertaken in two stages. Study 1 was carried out in the U.K. in 1990-1991 with eight children. Study 2 was carried out in Finland in 1991-1992 with thirty children. All the children were between 10 to 11 years old and were chosen for the studies according to their attainment levels in their first language, based primarily on teacher assessment. They has all used computers in their schools on a regular basis and were able to take full advantage of the word processing software employed in the study.

Eight children, four boys and four girls, from one English primary school participated in Study 1. Four were of low language attainment (two boys and two girls) and four of high language attainment (two boys and two girls). They worked in pair groups consisting of one boy and one girl and these mixed-gender pair groups were either of uniform or mixed attainment. In this study, eight group compositions were studied in which the same child participated in two kinds of attainment groups, uniform and mixed attainment groups. This made it possible to compare the same pupil's oral language in two different attainment groupings.

Study 2 involved thirty children, ten low attainment (5 girls and 5 boys), ten average attainment and ten high attainment children from a Finnish primary school. This study focused on low attainment children's language use in uniform and mixed attainment groups.

Methods

Data was gathered through observations, interviews, tape recordings, transcripts and through a system of analysis which classifies children's talk into categories according to its functions.

All the studied pair groups had a common goal at the word processor: to write together in a reciprocal way about topics commonly used for writing practices in their schools. Children were allowed to devise their writing activities at the word processors for themselves. The time allowed for writing at the word processor was not set beforehand and each pair group was permitted to complete their writing task.

A direct observation method was employed in order to understand better the language interactions. This included recording information about the writing task and about the materials children were able to use during their time at the computer as well as their non-verbal behaviour. All language interactions between children in each pair group were tape-recorded to get a full and permanent record of the talk. Each pair group was tape-recorded once for about a half an hour and all the tape recordings were transcribed.

In order to gain a better understanding of the reasons why certain language functions occurred in children's talk, all the children were interviewed after they had finished their collaborative writing task at the computer. The questions posed to children mostly concerned their attitudes to word processors, to writing, to collaborative activities, and towards their partner in the group. Sometimes children were also asked to give reasons for their particular uses of language.

The talk produced was analysed using a functional analysis system. This interpretative system is based on socio-cognitive theories which emphasize the importance of studying language use and mental processes in socio-cultural settings (Vygotsky, 1978; Wertsch, 1991). The approach is based on the notion that there exists a close relationship between social communicative processes and individual psychological processes. In this sense the use of the functional system allows one to investigate the thought processes which underlie the different uses of language (Phillips, 1988). In addition, it facilitates an examination of the reasons why particular uses of language are used in particular social settings.

The most comprehensive analysis system which classifies children's talk into categories according to functions is that developed by Fourlas (Fourlas, 1988; Fourlas & Wray, 1990). This categorisation system emerged from the collected data of children's verbal interactions in classroom learning contexts and is usable for investigations of both whole class teaching and small group discussions. In the system each language utterance is believed to carry various meanings and to reflect children's thinking processes. In order to make the classification system more applicable for the purposes of the present study, it was necessary to develop it somewhat during a pilot-study.

The functions identified in Fourlas' system are Informative (I), Compositional (C), Interrogative (Q), Judgemental (J), Organisational (OR), External thinking (ET), Responsive (R), Reproductional (RP), Affectional (AF), Argumentational (ARG), Expositional (EXPO), Heuristic (HE), Experiential (E), Hypothetical (HY), Imaginative (IM) and Intentional (IN). A more detailed description of the system can be seen in Appendix 1.

The Use of Language Functions at the Word Processor

From the data from Study 1 and 2, it appears that the general distribution of language functions was rather similar between the studies. The Informative, Interrogative, Organisational and Judgemental functions all occurred most frequently in both studies (Study 1: 54.2%, Study 2: 56.4%). The Responsive, Reproductional and Argumentational functions also had a similar frequency in both of the studies (Study 1: 17.0%, Study 2: 14.5%). Functions which occurred infrequently in both studies, accounting for less than 3% of the talk, were the Expositional, Hypothetical, Experiential, Heuristic and Imaginative functions. The Intentional function did not occur in either of the studies.

Some differences can be noted in children's use of language functions between the studies. One of these differences was the use of the Compositional function. In Study 1 it covered 13.4% of children's talk whereas in Study 2 it covered 9.3%. Among the other functions that differed quite notably in their distribution between the two studies were the Affectional (Study 1: 3.7%, Study 2: 9.5%) and the External thinking functions (Study 1: 8.1%, Study 2: 4.3%).

The reasons for the differences identified in the children's use of language functions between the studies can be many. One of them may be found in the topics of the children's writing (Fourlas, 1988). On the other hand, it should also be remembered that in Study 1 the data was gathered from both high and low attainment children whereas in Study 2 it came only from low attainment children. The differences notwithstanding, however, the similarities between the two studies appear to be significant in trying to understand the nature of children's learning experiences as represented in their talk during the process of collaborative writing at the computer.

Discussion

The findings suggest, on the whole, that the context created by the use of word processors for collaborative writing helped children to use their oral language and thinking for a variety of purposes. In the following discussion those language functions that occurred most frequently in the children's talk will be described in more detail.

The use of the Informative function

The frequent use of the Informative function shows that children were providing information based on their own knowledge and opinions, or were deriving it from the resources they had under their control, such as the word processor.

e.g.
1. Jaine: If you put a full stop there you don't need and.
2. Jaine: You can't do that because there is a full-stop.

3. Jaine: No, it's not moving. All the other letters are big and 'a's have gone small.

The use of the Informative function gives evidence of children reconstructing their knowledge through their talk. In sharing their understanding through verbal interaction, children were able to make connections between their own and their partner's knowledge and to explore issues mutually. Moreover, this may have helped children to construct new notions that went beyond their individual knowledge and hence enabled them to work in their zone of proximal development.

The use of the Interrogative function

From the data it is also interesting to note that the Interrogative function occurred in children's talk in great quantity. The use of this function gives evidence of children's intellectual curiosity. Through questioning children were attempting to make sense of their current activities. In this sense children can be characterized as having been actively involved in their own learning (Wells, 1987). Moreover, the high proportion of the Interrogative function suggests that children were relying on each other as information sources. This again indicates a high level of collaboration between the children.

e.g.
1. Kevin: What else do you want to write? How do you start a letter?
2. Owen : How do you spell that?
3. Gavin: Pick green now, yeah? This is not so fancy as yellow, is it?

Although the use of Interrogative function is important in terms of facilitating the exchange of children's knowledge, its use may not always encourage long-term planning or thoughtful opinion if viewed from the receiver's point of view. Instead, as can be seen from the examples given above, the use of Interrogative function can easily direct children's thoughts to certain specific areas and this may not necessarily foster children's 'higher order thinking' (Phillips, 1988).

Comparing the frequency of the Interrogative and the Responsive functions it can be noted that the Interrogative function was used more frequently. This suggests that children were not always requiring information or help from their peer in the group but just social approval. It also gives further evidence of a high level of collaboration among the children at the computer. The smaller amount of responses, on the other hand, may also have been due to the children's lack of ability to give answers to the questions posed by their peers. Nevertheless, questions posed during the process of collaborative writing may have helped children to identify gaps in their own knowledge. Questioning can thus be regarded as having a role to play in assisting children's learning.

The use of the Organisational function

The use of the Organisational function within the pair groups at the word processor was also notable. This provides further evidence of children being in charge of their own working and learning. Children were responsible for deciding the pattern of turn-taking and organising their work at the word processor. Children using their language in the Organisational function were reporting on present actions and hence not reflecting on the past or speculating about the future. Instead, children were using their language to regulate their own or their peer's behaviour.

e.g.
1. *Gavin: Let's go down here. Just carry on down, down....*
2. *Vicky: Let's try a different colour there. Let's swop places.*
3. *Jaine: And a full stop there. Let's write a little bit more down here.*

The high occurrence of the Organisational function indicates that the word processing context fostered quite procedural ways of thinking. Although this type of language use is important for children in order to solve problems and advance in their work, it does not necessarily require disembedded ways of thinking (Grieve and Hughes, 1990).

The use of the Judgemental function

The high proportion of the Judgemental function found in the children's talk suggests that children were not afraid of expressing their own opinions and views.

e.g.
1. *Katie: I know what we could do. (starts to write)*
2. *Kevin: Oh, not that.*
3. *Danny: We shouldn't have started like that.*

Although the Judgemental function occurred sometimes together with other functions, such as the Informative, Argumentational or Hypothetical function, it appears from the data that most of the time children used the Judgemental function on its own and hence did not justify their opinions in discussions. Previous research which has studied the connection between small group work interaction and learning outcomes in computer contexts has indicated that giving and receiving explanations can support learning whereas language use without reasoning may not lead to cognitive change. In fact, from the receiver's point of view, the lack of justification and explanation is considered as possibly detrimental to learning (Jackson, et al, 1992; Nastasi & Clements, 1992). According to these arguments, the cognitive value of the use of the Judgemental function without justification remains questionable.

Phillips (1988), trying to explain the infrequent use of the Argumentational function in young children's talk suggests that children at the age of 10 to 12 appear to be just developing their skills in justifying opinions and constructing arguments. For him, children at this age may not be aware of the need to justify their opinions through discourse, although they may be able to do it in their minds. Learning to use arguments is, he argues, a slow and gradual process. In this sense Phillips sees the Judgemental function as a pre-stage towards the use of the Argumentational function of language. This may in part explain the low occurrence of the Argumentational and perhaps Hypothetical uses of language functions in the present study.

The use of the Compositional function

The high proportion of the use of the Compositional function indicates that the word processing context helped children to use their talk as a means of developing the meaning of their writing. Children were exploring new ways of expressing themselves. They were revising the text, either spoken or written, and in this way adding, extending or qualifying the text's range of application. In addition, children dictating writing to their peers were often organising the work at the computer.

e.g.
1. Owen: How can you tell about the snow... (thinking). Here it is snowing...
2. Jaine: Or over in England it is snowing.
3. Owen: The snow is pure white and freezing cold.

Wells (1987) emphasises the importance of stories and storying in education. For him, storying does not only contribute to the acquisition of literacy, but it is also the most fundamental means for making meaning and gaining control over the world. In this sense, he regards storying as an activity that covers all aspects of learning.

The use of the Reproductional function

The use of the Reproductional function also occurred frequently in both of the studies. The Reproductional function shows a high level of task involvement in that it refers to children reading their written text or repeating what had just been said. Moreover, it suggests that a word processing context had encouraged children to read and proof-read their writing. Although the use of this function can be seen as assisting children's language development, its use may not necessarily foster children's abstract ways of thinking. As with the use of the Organisational function, it appears not to suggest long term planning but rather very context specific ways of thinking.

e.g.
1. *Katie: That does not make any sense really. (starts to read the text) We would go on a holiday....*
2. *Vicky: Carrot for the nose. (creating text)*
3. *Danny: Yeah, and a carrot for the nose.*

The effect of task division at the word processor on children's talk

The data from both studies suggests that task division at the word processor was linked with children's use of language functions and modes of thinking. The following example clearly demonstrates the effect of task division on children's talk.

Here, Vicky is using the keyboard. Danny, who is sitting beside Vicky, seems to be heavily involved in creating and dictating the text as well as giving information. Vicky, on the other hand, appears to be more involved in organising the contents of the writing and hence focussing on more procedural matters.

Danny: Full stop. I wish that we would have snow over the Christmas holidays. Do they have a Christmas holiday, a six week holiday?
Vicky: What about ice-skating on the snow?
Danny: No, that's not snow. That's ice. Well...hmm...
Vicky: Let's put something about ice.
Danny: Ice is made out of snow.
Vicky: Ice... (starts to write)
Danny: We like to ice-skate on it. Do they know what ice-skating is ? Ice skating is... (interrupted)
Vicky: Wait a minute.

As can be seen from the example the use of the keyboard appeared to encourage children to concentrate on contextually-embedded, or procedural, interactions in contrast to those of non-keyboarding children. Furthermore, use of the keyboard seemed to decrease the range of children's language functions.

General Discussion

From the data it appears that word processors may add an important dimension to the collaborative writing process by encouraging children to articulate plans and reactions about their writing. Through verbal interaction children in peer groups were not only found to come to terms with what they knew, but seemed to create a discussion in which knowledge was constructed as negotiable. From the distribution pattern of language functions, it also appears that children in small groups were able to create intersubjectivity and thus facilitate the exchange of each other's knowledge through oral interaction. Furthermore, the word processing context appeared to offer a conversational setting that enabled children to use their language for various functions which itself can be seen as important in assisting children's language development (Donaldson, 1978; Phillips, 1988; Wells, 1987).

The high amount of on-task talk indicates that the word processing context did foster children's collaboration with each other. It also shows that children were able to rely on themselves as information sources rather than seeking assistance from elsewhere. Similar findings have been reported from other studies concerned with group work at computers (see Hall & Rhodes, 1986; Keith & Glover, 1987; Hill & Browne, 1988). Yet, the high amount of on-task talk at the word processor appeared not to be connected with 'high quality interactions'. Instead, the findings of the present study imply that the environment created by the use of computers encouraged children to focus on procedural ways of thinking. For example, the Imaginative, Hypothetical, Experiential and Heuristic functions hardly occurred in children's language interactions at the word processor. Nonetheless, they are the functions characterized as reflecting exploratory ways of learning (Barnes, 1976; Phillips, 1990), and regarded as important in fostering abstract ways of thinking (Britton, 1972). This finding contradicts arguments which hold that content-free tools such as word processors have the potential to encourage the use of sophisticated functions like imagining and hypothesizing (see Dudley-Marling & Searle, 1989).

The data from this research also suggests that there may be a whole range of other factors that can affect the nature of children's interactions at word processors. Among them are those connected with group composition, namely task division at the word processor. Children's attainment level and gender were also found to be linked with children's talk. On the other hand, it should also be noted that the reasons for children's contextually-embedded uses of language, especially during the use of the keyboard, may not only be connected with the use of word processors, but also with the ways in which the children were accustomed to using their language in both home and school. As a consequence, it appears to be important not to view word processors as individual, separate tools from classroom contexts. Instead, they should be seen as a part of classroom culture interacting with many other factors in the social contexts of classrooms.

In order to encourage children to use their oral language more frequently in exploratory and abstract ways at word processors, it seems important to pay attention to teachers' ways of promoting children's language use in classrooms. Children should be made aware of the importance of using their language in ways which facilitate the development of their 'higher order thinking skills'. Attention should also be paid to planning small group work activities at word processors. This would include paying careful attention to the actual procedures that children undergo during the process of collaborative writing. Also the organisation of children at computers should be carefully planned. Moreover, the roles children and teachers can take during small group activities needs to be taken into consideration.

Conclusions

Although the findings of the present study indicate that a word processing context is not highly successful in encouraging children to use language and to think in disembedded ways, it may be that collaborative discussions at the computer still offered children opportunities to learn. For Vygotsky (1978), learning is not a simple process but rather a complex and dialectical one which he characterises by periodicity and unevenness. In this sense Vygotsky sees learning as being a non-linear process. Relating his views to the findings of the current study it may be that children might have profited from collaborating around the word processor although they were not clearly showing it. On the other hand, it should also be acknowledged that most of the children attending primary schools today are in the process of learning to use word processors. Moreover, many of them are also learning to use their oral language as a means for exploration and reflection. Thus at this stage the quality of their language interactions is likely to be quite context specific and procedural. What the nature of their learning experiences at word processors will be like in the near future can be seen as one of the aims of further research.

References

Barnes, D. (1976) *From Communication to Curriculum*, Harmondsworth: Penguin

Barnes, D. & Todd, F. (1977) *Communication and Learning in Small Groups*, London: Routledge and Kegan Paul Ltd

Britton, J. (1972) *Language and Learning*, Harmondsworth: Penguin Books.

Campbell, D. (1988) 'A Case-study of Computer Aided Writing in a Primary School', *Micro Scope Special*, Newman College with MAPE, pp. 9-18.

Cazden, C., John, V. & Hymes, D. (Eds) (1972) *Functions of Language in the Classroom*, Colombia University, USA: Teachers College Press

Cochran-Smith, M. (1991) 'Word Processing and Writing in Elementary Classrooms: A Critical Review of Related Literature', *Review of Educational Research*, Vol. 61, No. 1, pp. 107-155.

Dickinson, D. (1986) 'Cooperation, Collaboration, and a Computer: Integrating a Computer into a First-Second Grade Writing Program', *Research in the Teaching of English*, Vol. 20, No. 4, pp. 357-378.

Donaldson, M. (1978) *Children's Minds*, London: Fontana

Dudley-Marling, C. & Searle, D. (1989) 'Computers and Language Learning: Misguided Assumptions', *British Journal of Educational Technology*, Vol. 20, No. 1, pp. 41-46.

Fourlas, G. (1988) *A Comparative Study of the Functions of Children's Oral Language in Teacher Centered and Peer Group Centered Methods of Teaching in Greek Primary Schools.* Unpublished MEd thesis. University College Cardiff.

Fourlas, G. & Wray, D. (1990) 'Children's oral language: a comparison of two classroom organisational systems', in Wray, D. (ed) *Emerging Partnerships: Current Research in Language and Literacy* Clevedon: Multilingual Matters

Grieve, R. & Hughes, M. (Ed) (1990) *Understanding Children*, Oxford: Basil Blackwell

Hall, J. & Rhodes, V. (1986) *Microcomputers in Primary Schools - some observations and recommendations for good practice*, Educational Computing Unit, Centre for Educational Studies, King's College, London.

Hill, A. & Browne, A. (1988) 'Talk and the microcomputer: an investigation in the infant classroom', *Reading*, Vol. 22, No. 1, pp. 61-69 (See also this volume).

Hooper, S., Ward, T., Hannafin, M. & Clark, H. (1989) 'The Effects of Aptitude Composition on Achievement during Small Group Learning', *Journal of Computer Assisted Instruction*, Vol. 16, No. 3, pp. 102-109.

Hughes, M. (1990) 'Children's Computation,' in Grieve, R. & Hughes, M. (Ed) *Understanding Children*, Oxford: Basil Blackwell

Jackson, A., Fletcher, B. & Messer, D. (1992) 'When Talking Doesn't Help: An Investigation of Microcomputer-Based Group Problem Solving,' *Learning and Instruction*, Vol. 2, pp. 185-197.

Keith, G. & Glover, M. (1987) *Primary Language Learning with Microcomputers*, Beckenham: Croom Helm

King, A. (1989) 'Verbal Interaction and Problem-solving within Computer Assisted Cooperative Learning', *Educational Computing Research*, Vol. 5, No. 1, pp. 1-15

Light, P. (1987) 'Collaborative Interactions at the Microcomputer Keyboard', *Educational Psychology*, Vol. 7, No. 1, pp. 13-22.

Nastasi, B. & Clements, D. (1992) 'Socio-Cognitive Behaviours and Higher-Order Thinking in Educational Computer Environments', *Learning and Instruction*, Vol. 2, pp. 215-238.

Peacock, M. & Breese, C. (1990) 'Pupils with Portable Writing Machines', *Educational Review*, Vol. 42, No. 1, pp. 41-56.

Phillips, T. (1988) 'Why Successful Small-Group Talk Depends upon Not Keeping to the Point', In MacLure, M., Phillips, T. & Wilkinson, A. (Eds) *Oracy Matters*, Milton Keynes: Open University Press

Phillips, T. (1990) 'Structuring Contexts for Exploratory Talk', In Wray, D. (Ed) *Talking and Listening*, Leamington Spa: Scholastic

Robinson, B. (1985) *Microcomputers and the Language Arts*, Milton Keynes: Open University Press

Sutherland, R. & Hoyles, C. (1987) *Ways of learning: Insights about children, computers and mathematics in a LOGO environment*, University of London, Institute of Education.

TIzard, B. & Hughes, M. (1984) *Young Children Learning*, London: Fontana.

Vygotsky, L. (1978) *Mind in Society*, Cambridge, MA.: Harvard University Press.

Wells, G. (1987) *The Meaning Makers* Oxford: Heinemann

Wertsch, J. (1991) *Voices of the Mind*, New York: Simon & Schuster

Appendix 1.

Brief Description of the Functions of Children's Oral Language

Informative: Providing information, either by manipulating information resources or from previous ideas or knowledge
Compositional: Creating written or spoken text not earlier mentioned, revising previous formulations or dictating to a peer
Interrogative: Asking a question in order to get information or social approval
Judgemental: Expressing agreement or disagreement
Organisational: Organising tasks or behaviour
External thinking: Thinking aloud in accompaniment of a task
Responsive: Answering questions
Reproductional: Reproducing previously encountered language either by reading or repeating
Affectional: Expression of personal feelings
Argumentational: Reasoning in language
Expositional: Language accompanying the demonstration of a phenomena
Heuristic: Expressing discovery
Experiential: Expressing personal experiences
Hypothetical: Putting forward a hypotheses
Imaginative: Introducing or expressing imaginative situations
Intentional: Seeking permission or signalling intention to participate

Computer applications in the identification and remediation of dyslexia

Chris Singleton

The lack of general availability of facilities for identifying dyslexics, especially at an early age, can be a problem for many teachers and psychologists. The teacher may have pupils who are encountering "unexpected" difficulties in acquiring literacy skills, but not have ready access to facilities or techniques which could confirm or disconfirm dyslexia. The psychologist may have insufficient time to carry out detailed assessments of all children with literacy problems at an early age. Consequently, such children are often left until they are lagging so far behind their peers that the problem must be addressed, by which time the experience of repeated failure and frustration will almost certainly have seriously eroded these children's motivation and self-confidence.

Dyslexia is not just a difficulty with reading: it can affect the range of literacy skills as well as aspects of numeracy. But dyslexia also extends much wider than this, because it is essentially a problem with the way in which the brain organises, stores and processes certain types of information. Current research evidence indicates that in most cases the condition is of genetic origin but where there is no clear indication of a family history of literacy difficulties, birth difficulties are frequently found to be the most likely cause of the problem. (see Pavlidis, 1990, for reviews). Since it is an information processing dysfunction it not only affects the child before he or she starts school, it also persists into adult life, although as dyslexics get older they generally becomes more adept at circumventing their difficulties. At school, however, the difficulty cannot be circumvented because it invariably impairs the acquisition of basic skills to a greater or lesser degree. Without those basic skills dyslexics are unable to access the curriculum to the extent to which their intelligence requires, and they often become increasingly frustrated and resentful because they cannot understand why learning some things is so difficult for them but apparently so easy for others.

The purpose of current research on computer-based techniques for identification of dyslexia is to equip the teacher with techniques for clarifying a child's difficulties as early as possible, so that appropriate educational provision can be made more easily. The computer can also be used to provide backup to a structured programme of literacy teaching, giving valuable extra practice in component skills of reading and spelling as well as facilitating the development of structure and creativity in writing.

The rationale for early identification of dyslexia

The early identification of unexpected learning difficulties is a very attractive goal, both educationally and socially, but a difficult task (Pumfrey and Reason, 1991; Singleton, 1988). Arguably, identification of those who are "at risk" of learning difficulties, implies assessment before the child has evidenced failure in the learning task. It presumes that we can measure the relevant underlying cognitive dysfunctions with reasonable accuracy while the child is still "at risk" but before those dysfunctions have hindered the child's learning. Moreover, it implies a screening approach, since if failure has not yet occurred, there is no basis for selection of children for assessment. Leaving aside for the moment the problems of the content of such assessment procedures, the sheer practicalities of universal screening of, say, five-year-olds for potential learning difficulties would be a daunting task. Who would carry it out? It is apparent that the educational psychology and learning support services would not have the means to carry out such a programme without massive increases in personnel. That leaves only the classroom teacher, who many would argue is already so overburdened with assessment duties that teaching activities are seriously threatened.

A particularly attractive solution would seem to lie in the use of computer technology, which is capable not only of countering the two problems just mentioned but also has the added advantage of affording superior accuracy in measurement. The precision, objectivity and flexibility of the computer makes it an ideal tool for assessing cognitive abilities and deficits. What would the nature of such a computer screening package be? To answer this question it is necessary to examine our knowledge of the cognitive precursors of dyslexic difficulties.

Predicting reading difficulties

It has long been known that sub-test profiles of individual intelligence scales can often reveal some of the cognitive deficits of dyslexics, although the subject has not been without its controversies (Thomson, 1990; Tyler and Elliott, 1988). When contrasted with the general depression of scores across sub-tests shown by the "slow learner", such profiles indicate that the typical areas of deficit for the dyslexic are in memory (verbal, or visual, or both), sequencing, phonological processing, and overall speed of information processing. Experimental studies of the cognitive deficits of developmental dyslexics have confirmed this view (see Singleton, 1987, for review).

It is now well established that various phonological processing abilities are very closely related to reading development (for a review see Goswami and Bryant, 1990). For example, children who, when they start school, show good awareness of the components of spoken language and a capacity for analysing these are the ones who are most likely to make good progress in learning to read. On the other hand, children with difficulty in carrying out these types of phonological tasks when they begin school are the ones who are most likely to have difficulties with learning to read even though they may overcome their difficulties with speech sounds as such. There is now substantial evidence that, in particular, skill in the phonological processes involved in rhyme and alliteration predicts reading development independently of intelligence and social background, and that children with difficulties in these aspects of cognitive activity are more likely than others to have subsequent problems in learning to read and spell.

Of the ongoing research projects on phonological awareness in this country, two are of particular interest in the search for effective techniques for early identification of dyslexia. At the School of Education, University of Birmingham, a research group are investigating phonological awareness in pre-school children, incorporating a training programme to compensate for some children's lack of experience, with long-term follow-up of the literacy development of a target group (see Layton and Upton, 1992). In Suffolk, three Learning Support Advisory Teachers are investigating the effects of a pre-school "Rhyme Curriculum" on phonological development and subsequent reading progress (Kerr, Buckley and James, 1992). Although both of these projects are in their early stages, both are beginning to produce data which confirms the importance of phonological awareness activities in the pre-school and infant curriculum.

When good and poor readers of matched overall I.Q. are compared on various psychological measures we typically find differences in underlying cognitive functions subserving memory, phonological processing and sequencing skills (Ellis and Large, 1987; Jorm, Share, MacLean and Matthews, 1986). When non-verbal I.Q. alone is controlled in comparison between dyslexic and non-dyslexic subjects, the groups are found to differ only on verbal memory and rapid naming ability (Bowers et al., 1988). But when verbal I.Q. alone is controlled, differences which show up between the groups tend to be associated with visual and orthographic defects (Willows, 1990). Thus although a substantial body of research has demonstrated that reading difficulties are, in general, most strongly linked to a wide variety of verbal deficits (Perfetti, 1985) and consequently such deficits are likely to be encountered much more frequently than deficits in visual-perceptual abilities (Lovegrove and Slaghuis, 1989) it is important that early identification procedures, as well as tapping underlying verbal deficits, should also take account of any possible visual or orthographic defects. In summary, therefore, we can propose that the underlying componential skills in early reading development fall into three broad areas. These areas are: verbal abilities (including phonological awareness), visual/perceptual abilities, and memory processes. These components overlap so that differential deficits will result in a different pattern of impairment in componential skills and a different profile of literacy difficulties.

Computer based identification of dyslexia

The feasibility of computer-based assessment techniques in dyslexia was demonstrated in the late 1980's in a number of pioneering studies reviewed by Singleton (1991c and 1992a). More recently, two projects in Britain are of particular note. At the University of Sheffield, Nicolson, Fawcett and Pickering are developing a suite of diagnostic programs known as "DEST" (Dyslexia Early Screening Test) for low-cost screening of schoolchildren, using the HyperCard environment available on Apple Macintosh computers (see Fawcett, Pickering and Nicolson (1992). This project embraces a global approach to the problem of finding the best predictors of dyslexia, so that various computerised tests are being used in conjunction with items from more conventional tests.

At the University of Hull a major research project to develop computer techniques for the early identification of dyslexia has been funded by Humberside County Council. The software created for the Humberside project includes many different tests of associative and sequential memory in both verbal and visual/perceptual modes, as well as measures of verbal and visual analytical processes, such as auditory discrimination and transient channel response. These are being administered to a large sample of 5 year-olds in 24 schools across the County of Humberside. The children will be followed through over several years to examine early literacy development in relation to their performance on the computer tests. All the programs are in the format of "games" which the children usually find to be very enjoyable, and are administered in the classroom in short sessions so that the children do not become tired or lose concentration. Comparison data are also being obtained from a sample of older children who have already been diagnosed as dyslexic.

However, it is important to note that the Humberside project is not attempting to label children as "dyslexic" at the age of five years on the basis of a battery of computer tests. The aim of this project is to produce an easy-to-use computer-based package of tests which will give early indication of many of the children who are at risk of literacy difficulties because of underlying cognitive deficits, who might not otherwise be spotted until very much later in their school careers. It is intended that the package should ultimately be made available in versions suitable for the full range of machines commonly used in schools as well as versions which would utilise various input devices, such as concept keyboards and touch screens (see Singleton, 1991c, 1992a.) Without early identification procedures the teacher may easily assume that the child is lazy or simply requires more time for reading skills to "click". Obviously, however, the ultimate success of a project such as this depends largely upon the availability of teaching facilities in the schools which are appropriate to the needs of any child who which the test battery indicates is probably "at risk". For this reason, it is essential to increase the general provision of teaching staff in ordinary schools who can deliver carefully structured language-based teaching programmes for dyslexics, using multi-sensory techniques and embodying substantial amounts of overlearning.

Use of computers in the education of the dyslexic

Although dyslexics have many difficulties, the principal difficulty which the vast majority of dyslexics have to cope with is poor memory. According to current research evidence, what seems mainly to be at fault with the memory of the dyslexic are the processes which enable information to be transferred from short-term to long-term memory (see Torgesen, 1985, 1987). For the vast majority of learned activities this transfer is achieved by structuring the information appropriately and rehearsing it an adequate number of times. It is this ability to structure and rehearse information, then, which is essentially weak in the dyslexic. The key to successful teaching of the dyslexic, therefore, is the provision of maximum support, encouragement and opportunity for creating structure in learning and enabling ample practice to facilitate rehearsal processes (see Thomson and Watkins, 1991). The teacher can provide the former not only by efficient organisation of components of a learning module (e.g. a cumulative programme of phonics teaching) but also in the structuring of the overall learning programme. For example, the dyslexic with mainly verbal memory difficulties will generally be found to encounter problems in acquiring phonic skills, applying sound-to-spelling rules, and monitoring the "message" of what he or she is trying to convey in a piece of writing. By contrast, the dyslexic with mainly visual memory difficulties will tend to have problems in building up a sight vocabulary for efficient word recognition, remembering letter patterns in irregularly spelled words, and detection of errors in writing activities. The effective remediation programme needs to be structured to cater for these differences.

Where does the computer fit into all this? Firstly, the computer can provide dyslexics with opportunities for very much more practice at component skills than they would normally be able to get from other sources (Singleton, 1991d). Some of the most appropriate software falls into the "Drill and Practice" category and although there is a tendency in some quarters to deride such computer activities as being "uncreative and outmoded" nevertheless, because of the dyslexic's memory difficulties, they still have a most valuable part to play in computer work with dyslexics (Hutchins, 1991). In addition, there are an increasing range of computer activities which can enable dyslexics to learn how to structure their written work effectively and realise their creative potential in the written medium (for review see

Singleton, 1991, 1992b).

It is essential, however, that computer work is properly integrated within a well-structured programme of teaching. The computer does not replace the teacher, but extends the teacher's effectiveness. Computer software needs to be carefully chosen and used in such a way that the pupil has maximum opportunity for reinforcing new skills (Singleton, 1991b). As computers are becoming much more widely available in schools, they are being seen increasingly as a very cost-effective way of assisting the teacher in the time-intensive process of educating the dyslexic child, especially in providing opportunities for practice of basic skills. However, one should not overlook the substantial motivational benefits which computer activities have for dyslexic children. The computer is a non-critical, endlessly patient "teacher" which can provide interesting and varied activities which tend to increase the time children are willing to spend on literacy work. The active involvement of the child with the computer as a tool for the production of written work of varying sorts or as a problem-solving device (e.g. as with LOGO) also enables the learner to shape and control his or her own learning experience, thus enhancing the development of the individual's organisational and thinking skills.

References

Bowers, P., Steffy, R., & Tate, E. (1988) Comparison of the effects of IQ control methods on memory and naming speed predictors of reading disability. *Reading Research Quarterly,* 23, 304-319.

Ellis, N.C. & Large, B. (1987) The development of reading. *British Journal of Psychology,* 78, 1-28.

Fawcett, A.J., Pickering, S., & Nicolson, R.I. (1992) Development of the DEST test for the early screening for dyslexia. In R. Groner, R. Kaufmann-Hayoz, & S.F.Wright (Eds) *Reading and Reading Disorders: International Perspectives* North Holland/Elsevier.

Goswami, U. & Bryant, P. (1990) *Phonological skills and learning to read.* Laurence Erlbaum Associates.

Hutchins, J. (Ed.) (1991) *Computer Users' Bulletin* Dyslexia Computer Resource Centre, University of Hull, in association with the British Dyslexia Association.

Jorm, A.F., Share, D.L., MacLean, R. & Matthews, R. (1986) Cognitive factors at school entry predictive of specific reading retardation and general reading backwardness: a research note. *Journal of Child Psychology and Psychiatry,* 27, 45-54.

Kerr, A., Buckley, J., & James, F. (1992) *Rhyme: a resource for teachers of reading.* Suffolk County Council Education Department.

Layton, L. & Upton, G. (1992) Phonological training and the pre-school child. *Education,* 3, (13 March), 34-36.

Lovegrove, W. & Slaghuis, W. (1989) How reliable are visual differences found in dyslexics? *Irish*

Journal of Psychology, 10, 542-550.

Pavlidis, G. (Ed.) (1990) *Perspectives on Dyslexia.* 2 vols. New York: Wiley

PerfettI, C.A. (1985) *Reading Ability* New York: Oxford Univ. Press.

Pumfrey, P.D. & Reason, R. (1991) *Specific learning disabilities (Dyslexia)* London: NFER-Nelson.

Singleton, C.H. (1987) Dyslexia and cognitive models of reading. *Support for Learning,* 2, 47-56.

Singleton, C.H. (1988) The early diagnosis of developmental dyslexia. *Support for Learning,* 3, 108-121.

Singleton, C.H. (Ed.) (1991a) *Computers and Literacy Skills,* Dyslexia Computer Resource Centre, Univ. of Hull.

Singleton, C.H. (1991b) A rationale for computer-assisted literacy instruction. In Singleton (Ed.), *Computers and Literacy Skills,* Dyslexia Computer Resource Centre, Univ. of Hull, pp. 9 - 21.

Singleton, C.H. (1991c) Computer applications in the diagnosis and assessment of cognitive deficits in dyslexia. In Singleton (Ed.), *Computers and Literacy Skills,* Dyslexia Computer Resource Centre, Univ. of Hull, pp. 149 - 159.

Singleton, C.H. (1991d) *Developments in the use of computers for the diagnosis and remediation of cognitive deficits in dyslexia.* Paper presented at the Second International Conference of the British Dyslexia Association, Oxford, April 1991.

Singleton, C.H. (1992a) *The use of computers in the early identification of dyslexia.* Paper presented at the Fourth Helen Arkell Conference, Cambridge, April 1992.

Singleton, C.H. (1992b) The patient teacher. *Special Children,* Sept. 1992, 28-32.

Singleton, C.H. (1992c) Early identification of dyslexia. *Dyslexia Contact,* 11(2).

Thomson, M.E. (1990) *Developmental Dyslexia* Third Edition. London: Whurr.

Torgesen, J.K. (1985) Memory Processes in Reading Disabled Children *Journal of Learning Disabilities,* 18, 350-357.

Torgesen, J.K. et al. (1987) Academic difficulties of learning disabled children who perform poorly on memory span tasks. In H.L. Swanson (Ed.) *Memory and Learning Disabilities.* Greenwich, Conn: JAI Press, pp. 305-333.

Tyler, S. & Elliott, C.D. (1988) Cognitive profiles of poor readers and dyslexic children on the British Ability Scales. *British Journal of Psychology,* 79, 493-508.

Willows, D.M. (1990) Visual processes in learning disabilities. In B. Wong (Ed.) *Learning about Learning Disabilities* New York: Academic Press.

A review of the use of microcomputer software by teachers supporting pupils experiencing specific learning difficulties

Hamid Sepehr and Duncan Harris

Introduction

Despite the relatively extensive spread of the use of microcomputers in schools, studies of actual classroom practices are more limited. The researchers' focus on software design and experimental frameworks seems to have dominated heavily a field in great need of reflection and communication among practitioners. The research on the use of computers in reading instruction in particular seems to suffer from such shortcomings (Balajthy, 1989). In the field of Special Educational Needs (S.E.N.) greater focus on specific areas and learner groups seems to be required (e.g. HMI, 1991).

Our concern with the use of computers to support pupils with Specific Learning Difficulties (SpLDs) has led us to believe that studies of teaching practices may facilitate greater dialogue and awareness and encourage critical reflection. In this paper we wish to present some of the findings of an exploratory study into the use of microcomputer software by support teachers which may enable better practice and software design.

The general background

The concern with the quality and educational soundness of computer use is not new (e.g. Self, 1985; Balajthy, 1989, pp. 83-84). Kinzer *et al* (1986, p. 131) have discussed the ethical issues involved in considering the quality of computer software and its use in educational setting. Daniel Chandler (1990) alerts us to the 'educational ideology' of the computer software and more recently Preston (1992) has argued the case for a 'socially critical approach' to the use of computers in teaching. On reviewing the literature one is struck by how relatively scarce the research on teacher practice has been. Many of the existing studies have tended to point to rather important if not worrying outcomes. The following examples, predominantly from among the American research, may serve as pointers to issues of relevance.

The survey carried out by Becker and his colleagues at John Hopkins University in 1983 and repeated in 1985 is one of the most notable wide-scale surveys. In this study, elementary school teachers reported that 'drill and practice' activities accounted for 73% of computer time, and 'tutorial' instruction occupied a further

24% (Becker, 1986 in Balajthy, 1989, p. 84).

Squire (1985), reviewing the developments in reading software and their applications, found that: "not only do children from culturally different and economically handicapped background have fewer opportunities than their peers to interact with computers, but that what experience they do have is more than twice as likely to be limited to 'drill and practice' activities."

Other studies have included available software and sales. Reinking, Kling and Harper (1985) found that about 70% of reading software programs on the market involved 'drill and practice'. Robin and Bruce (1984) found that most of over 300 language arts programs surveyed were targeted to the letter or word level of language (Balajthy, 1989, p.85).

In a project involving teachers, mildly handicapped adolescents and administrators, Okolo *et al* (1989) employed interviews and comprehensive observational techniques to study the patterns of computer use in one district. They report that "the prominent use of the microcomputers were limited to mathematics, 'drill and practice' and games. Special educators and students did not view computers as having a significant impact on instructional practices and programs. Lack of access to microcomputers and dissatisfaction with existing software were cited as major barriers to more extensive and varied microcomputer use."

Such findings assume greater significance if the condition of pupils experiencing literacy difficulties is considered. A great portion of the recent research in reading has stressed the importance of meaningful and purposeful activities for learning (e.g. Wray and Medwell, 1991). Researchers within the field of 'reading difficulties' are also pointing to the need to assume new approaches. "Samuel T. Orton and his associates introduced powerful and lasting paradigms for dyslexia and learning disabilities. However, as any field advances, old paradigms are modified and new paradigms are being supplanted by collaborative, strategy-based paradigms" (Wigg 1991).

With this background, warnings about 'decontextualised' and 'meaningless' activities have been clear. Some 'drill and practice' computer programs have been singled-out as representing a potential for such 'decontextualisation' (Smith, 1988, Kinzer et al, 1986).

In Britain, the 'holistic' and 'active learning' approaches to reading have been closely associated with so called 'framework' or 'content-free' software. Such programs aim to represent flexible tools which could be shaped by teachers or learners to suit their needs. Wordprocessors, data-bases, some educational games and a number of programs following the 'cloze' framework are seen as exemplifying such 'category' of software and have been recommended by various authors (e.g. Kinzer et al, 1986; Wepner, 1989; Hope, 1986).

An HMI report (1990b) claimed that the development of literacy skills constitutes the area most widely and successfully supported by IT among pupils with S.E.N. A number of recent reports have nevertheless emphasised the need for a move in research and development towards the study of particular group needs (HMI, 1990a; HMI, 1990b; POST, 1991; NCET, 1991). In this context, the setting-up of specialist development groups by the NCET (NCET, 1991) including a working group on Specific Learning Difficulties (Dyslexia) are interesting developments.

A small-scale exploratory study

The findings reported in this paper have been part of a wider review of the understanding and means of using the computer to support pupils who experience specific learning difficulties (Sepehr, 1991). The study was undertaken in the Spring of 1991. Adopting a case-study approach (Stenhouse, 1982), questionnaire and interview techniques were used along with a review of the literature on the topic. The themes for the inquiry emerged from a pilot study of classroom observations and teacher interviews.

A total of 56 questionnaire returns and 9 focused, semi-structured interviews have been analysed. The interviews generally attempted to explore further the issues raised by the questionnaires. The interviewees were teachers who had already responded through the questionnaire.

As one of the authors works in Spain and has been on a study leave in Britain, we found it useful to include a small sample of Spanish teachers from Madrid. Their involvement has resulted in 6 questionnaire returns and one interview. The Spanish group of teachers could be regarded as representing teachers working mainly within a voluntary organisation and providing 'remedial support'; a small, but important group among the teachers particularly engaged in supporting pupils with SpLDs in this country as well as in Spain. The other respondents are all teachers from within LEAs in London. They include a small number of teachers from Special Schools and an equally small number of class teachers who support the specific needs of their pupils within their 'mainstream' classroom. The majority are teachers who have been attached to support services within LEAs and are often based in one school and may work within or outside of the classroom supporting pupils with S.E.N. The teachers' average length of experience is 10.8 years. A brief profile of pupils' age range and the teachers' involvement is presented in Table 1.

Pupils' age range	Number of teachers
3-6	2
5-7	29
8-11	35
11-14	38
14+	28

Table 1: Numbers of teachers and age-range taught

The teachers were asked if they had used the computer to support pupils with SpLD. Possible reasons for not using the computer were also elicited and the following likely reasons were suggested to them.

* lack of training
* shortage of teaching time
* preference for other methods
* lack of access
* lack of appropriate software
* other

A total of 17 teachers (30% of the respondents) reported that they had not used the computer (see Table 2 and Table 3). This percentage may be an underestimate if the irregular usage reported by most interviewees is taken into account.

	Number of teachers	% of respondents
Have used computer	38	69
Have not used computer	17	31

Table 2: Teachers use of the computer

	Number of references	% of non-users	% of respondents
Lack of training	6	35	11
Shortage of teaching time	9	53	16
Preference for other methods	8	47	14
Lack of access	10	59	18
Lack of appropriate software	4	23.5	7

Table 3: Teachers reasons for non-use of the computer

It was also considered interesting to suggest a possible link between the teachers' responses on 'shortage of time' and 'preference for other methods' with their concern regarding 'lack of appropriate software'. Given a scale of 1 to 5, and asked to make their perceived 'overall rating' of 'how widely they thought the computers were being used in this area', the teachers gave a mean rating of 2.1 (with 'users' scoring slightly higher than 'non-users'). When asked about their perception of the general 'effectiveness' and 'efficiency' (time related effectiveness) of microcomputer user, the teachers gave the respective mean ratings of 3.9 and 3.4.

The teachers were asked to name titles of software they had used in supporting literacy skills, to rate each one, and to specify their reasons for the use of that software. Hence, a list of some 72 software titles with teachers' ratings and criteria for use was compiled. The programmes referred to frequently were identified and are presented in Table 4. The table lists the number of references which were made to each software title.

Software title	Number of references
Phases	8
Tray	7
Folio	6
Caxton/ Caxton Press	5
Developing Tray	5
An Eye for Spelling	4
Blackwell Spelling	4
Star Spell Plus	4
"Wordprocessor"	3
Write	3

Table 4: Software titles most frequently mentioned

The teachers' reasons for the use of the software (Table 5) appear to merit greater attention. On the questionnaires, most teachers chose to present their reasons in the form of brief comments or single words. These comments have been edited and grouped together according to the core concepts that they represented. The potential qualitative significance of the comments should not be ignored. The most frequently cited comments are listed here in order of the frequency in which they were mentioned by the teachers.

Some of these comments were elaborated upon within the interviews. The interviews revealed clearly that many teacher constructs (e.g. 'motivation' or 'developing language skills') are understood in significantly different ways by different teachers (Kinzie and Berdel, 1990; Balajthy, 1989; Anderson-Inman, 1988-89). Such diversity in understanding is also found within the literature (e.g. Singleton, 1991; Hope, 1986; Kinzer et al, 1986).

As a means of creating a link with teachers' overall educational 'beliefs and practices' and in order to further expose the study to the general debate on literacy teaching and learning, a question on teachers' preferred general approach was included in the questionnaire (see Table 6). The categories suggested to the teachers ('whole book', 'structured phonics', etc) were extracted from a range of existing (and often confusing) terms used within the literature. Despite the existence of conflicting views on the subject, the terms seem to have been understood by the sample of teachers. While some teachers gave no response, others chose to signal to more than one option (e.g. 'structured phonics' as well as 'eclectic'). The responses are therefore analysed and presented (in Table 6) terms of number of references made (rather than number of teachers).

Comment	Frequency
Motivation	22
Drill/practice/repetition	13
Presentation/visual format	8
Group work/co-operation	7
Own word/own text	6
Developing language skills	5
Other material/backup activity	5
Game-like	5
Cross curricular/topic work	4
Drafting/editing	4
Problem solving	4
Creative writing/free writing	3
Levels of difficulty/progression	3
Sequencing	3
Enjoyment	2
Spinoff activities	2

Table 5: Most frequent teacher comments in software evaluation

	Number of references	% of responses
Whole book	9	16
Structured phonics	17	30
Eclectic	26	46
Other	5	9

Table 6: Preferred approach to literacy teaching

In terms of the software characteristics, a total of 64 program titles, mentioned by the teachers, were directly available and could be individually studied. These programs were then grouped under the two categories of 'framework' and 'drill and practice'. The difficulties involved in categorising some of the programs should be recognised.

Some teachers chose to name more than one software title. As a result, the 64 programs received 100 references. The findings on software categories are therefore presented in terms of the total number of program titles as well as the number of times they were referred to by the teachers (Table 7).

	Titles	%	Refs	%
Drill and practice	34	53	39	39
Framework	30	47	61	61
Total	64		100	

Table 7: Teachers' references to software types

It can be observed that, despite the slightly smaller number of 'framework' programs, they received a significantly higher number of references. It may also be interesting to note that the 'framework' programs covered a rather limited range and variety. In our accumulated list, they seem to include wordprocessors, desktop-publishers, 'cloze' activity programs and data bases. Some authors have, for its versatility, included the language LOGO among this software group too. Concept keyboards were also cited repeatedly by the teachers but have not appeared in our list as it was argued that they were better understood as 'interface' tools normally used with some of the wordprocessing packages already mentioned. Other recent and promising innovations such as the 'hypermedia' and 'voice-synthesizers' were not mentioned.

It is also interesting to note that a relatively high number of references to 'framework' software is made within a teacher population which appears to show a relative inclination towards 'structured' approaches to literacy teaching. A closer scrutiny of the questionnaires and the interviews also reveals that:

(a) teachers adhering to a 'whole book' approach rarely made any references to 'drill and practice' programmes and clearly preferred the 'framework' type.

(b) although the greater part of the references made to 'drill and practice' programs came from teachers preferring 'structured' or 'eclectic' approaches, they nevertheless made frequent references to 'framework' software.

Final words

It is hoped that the limited scope of the study, despite its limited scope, has been able to raise a number of questions on the topic and highlight the need for further research. We tend to agree with the view that when "technology and research are brought closer to teaching" (Kerr, 1990), the cycles of "evaluation for innovation" may stand a better chance of avoiding "alienation" and a "mismatch between the learner and content or approach to learning" (Harris and Bell, 1990).

A closer scrutiny of actual classroom practices and a larger sample of teachers are clearly needed. However, and perhaps more importantly, the learners' perspective should not be ignored. In this context, recent studies of learners' experiences of classroom use of the computer (e.g. Kirkman, 1993) should be particularly welcomed.

References

Anderson-Inman, L. (ed) (1988-89) 'Misconceptions about Reading and Software development' in *The Computing Teacher* Dec/Jan 1988-89, pp. 27-28

Balajthy, E. (1989) *Computers and Reading: lessons from the past and technologies of the future.* Englewood Cliffs. NJ: Prentice Hall

Chandler, D. (1990) 'The Educational ideology of the computer' in *British Journal of Educational Technology* Vol. 21. No. 3. pp. 165-174

Clarke, R.E. & Salmon, G. (1986) 'Media in Teaching' in Wittrock, M.C. (ed) *Handbook of Research on Teaching.* New York: Macmillan

Harris, D. & Bell, C. (1990) *Evaluating and Assessing for Learning.* London: Kogan Page

HMI (1990a) *Special Needs Issues.* London: HMSO

HMI (1990b) *Information Technology and Special Educational Needs in Schools.* London: HMSO.

Hope, M. (Ed) (1986) *The Magic of the Micro: a resource for children with learning difficulties.* Warwick: Council for Educational Technology

Kerr, S.T. (1989) 'Technology, teachers, and the Search for School Reform' in *Educational Technology Research and Development.* Vol. 37. No. 4. pp. 5-17

Kirkman, C. (1993) 'Computer experience and the attitude of 12 year old students: implications for the UK National Curriculum' in *Journal of Computer Assisted Learning* 9. pp. 51-62.

Kinzer, C.K. (*et al*) (1986) *Computer Strategies for Education: Foundations and Content-Area Applications.* Columbus, Ohio: Merril Publishing

Kinzie, M.B. & Berder, R.L. (1990) 'Design and Use of Hypermedia Systems' in *Educational Technology Research and Development.* Vol. 38. No. 3. pp. 61-68.

NCET (1991) Special Educational Needs: BETT '91 - Seminar Notes. NCET

OKOLO, C.M. (et al) (1989) 'Microcomputer Implementation in Secondary Special Education Programs: A Study of Special Educators - Mildly Handicapped Adolescents and Administrators' Perceptives' in *Journal of Special Education.* Vol. 23. No. 1. pp. 107-117

POST (1991) *Technologies for Teaching: the Use of Technologies for Teaching and learning in Primary and Secondary Education, Vol.1.* The Parliamentary Science and Technology Information Foundation: Parliamentary Office for Science and Technology.

Preston, N. (1992) 'Computing and Teaching: a socially critical review' in *Journal of Computer Assisted Learning* 8. 1. pp. 49-56.

Self, J. (1985) *Microcomputers in Education: A Critical Appraisal of Education Software.* Brighton: Harvester Press

Sepehr, H. (1991) *An investigation into the Use of Microcomputer Software to support the Learning of Literacy Skills by Pupils with Specific Learning Difficulties.* Unpublished MEd dissertation: Brunel University.

Singleton, C. (ed) (1991) *Computer and Literacy Skills.* Hull: British Dyslexia Association Computer Resource Centre

Smith, F. (1988) *Reading.* Cambridge: Cambridge University Press

Squire, J.R. (1985) 'The Labour of Sisyphus: Achieving Excellence in Schooling' paper presented at The Annual meeting of the International Reading Association May 5-9 1985. New Orleans: International Reading Association.

Stenhouse, L. (1982) 'The conduct, analysis and reporting of case-study in educational research and evaluation' in Murphy, R. & Torrance, H. (eds). *Evaluating Education: Issues and Methods.* London: Harper & Rowe.

Wepner, S.B. (1989) 'Stepping forward with reading software' in *Journal of Reading, Writing and Learning Disabilities International,* Vol.5. pp. 61-83

Wigg, E.H. (1991) 'Language-Learning Disabilities: Paradigms for the Nineties' in *Annals of Dyslexia.* Vol.41. pp. 3-22.

Wray, D. and Medwell, J. (1991) *Literacy and Language in the Primary Years.* London: Routledge.

Students and hypertext: developing a new literacy for a new reading context

Mark A. Horney and Lynne Anderson-Inman

Reading teachers beware! There's a revolution afoot- a revolution which sees itself as "...the wave of the future, the next stage of civilization, the next stage of literature and a clarifying force in education ..." (Nelson, 1987, p. 0/2). The vehicle for this upheaval will be "hypertext," a form of electronic reading and writing. Hypertext is to serve as a window into the entire corpus of human literacy, and so liberate readers from the narrow halls of frozen "linear" text, dictated by distant and authoritarian authors, and held prisoner on static paper pages. Instead, readers will be free to "read, on computer screens, from vast libraries easily, the things we choose being clearly and instantly available to us, in a great interconnected web of writings and ideas." (Nelson, 1987, p. 1/2)

Beyond the hoopla, hypertext is actually the simple, and no so new, notion of "non-sequential writing," and, by implication, non-sequential reading. Ted Nelson, one of the original hypertext revolutionaries, finds examples of hypertext anywhere readers are "free to choose," even in something as ordinary as a magazine page "...with sequential text and inset illustrations and boxes ...", (p. 1/17). The real power of hypertext, though, comes when it is coupled with a computer, and Nelson has spent much of the last 25 years working to develop hypertext editing systems. Nelson is not alone in this. Since 1987, hypertext has become a significant topic in computer science, in technical writing, and in educational computing. It is definitely something for educators in general, and reading teachers especially, to investigate, to prepare for, and for them to exploit themselves. However, the development of hypertext faces many difficulties, not the least of which is that until recently almost all hypertext research has been devoted to hardware and software issues, i.e. just programming computers to perform hypertext operations. Much less effort has been expended on observing how readers, and students specifically, read in hypertext environments. The work presented here is an effort to remedy this.

The ElectroText Project

Since 1990, we have been working with Larry Lewin, a local middle school teacher, on The ElectroText Project. *ElectroText* (Enabling Technologies, Inc., 1988) is a hypertext authoring system developed as an extension to the Macintosh program HyperCard (Apple Computer, Inc., 1987). We have used ElectroText to create hypertext versions of two short stories which were then used by Lewin in his 8th grade (ages 13-14) language arts class. Our observations of these 17 students are the basis for the study results presented here. The two stories were *Louisa, Please Come Home*, by Shirley Jackson (1988), and *The Landlady*, by Roald Dahl (1978). In addition to the main text of each story, the hypertext versions included vocabulary support, prompted writing assignments, and self-monitoring questions. These reading support tools were intended to assist students in understanding the story and provide them with guided practice in active reading strategies, a focus of the reading curriculum. Students were able to page through the story text and gain access to these resources by pointing to various screen icons. They were free to use or ignore the resources as they saw fit, and another curriculum goal was to teach students to make such choices. It is this characteristic of reader independence which qualifies these materials as hypertext, although perhaps on a more limited scale than that envisioned by Nelson. (A more complete description of ElectroText can be found in Anderson-Inman, 1989, and more about the project in Horney & Anderson-Inman, 1992.)

The students read the stories over a period of several days after first holding a class discussion about story themes and receiving instruction in the operation of ElectroText. In addition to reading the stories, students were required to respond to several writing prompts. Some students spent as much as three hours with the materials, and others as little as 70 minutes. A gap of approximately one month separated students' reading of the first story from their reading of the second story. This time was used to modify the software, improving certain features which appeared to be problematic.

Data about the students' work were collected from audio tapes of the classroom, interviews with selected students, responses to the writing prompts, responses to paper and pencil essay questions, and from transcripts created by a computer monitoring program which recorded students' moment by moment activities. This last data source proved to be particularly rich and allowed our research team to construct detailed accounts of how each student interacted with the computer. We developed several techniques to work with these data, including visual displays, called "Action Charts". These charts provide a graphic overview of student's experience with hypertext stories. The charts show each "event," i.e. some action performed by a reader, as a vertical bar. The heights of the bars indicate the type of action. Bars above zero represent events occurring among pages of the story, such as the start or ending of a work session (the longest bars), or movement from one page to another. The heights of these movement bars indicate what page of text, or which resource is being accessed. Bars below zero indicate events within a page, such as viewing a definition, asking self-monitoring questions, and opening "pop-ups". Pop-ups are a hypertext mechanism whereby a "text field," normally hidden, can be flashed onto the screen. These fields provide students with information, ask questions, and store student responses. Two types of pop-ups are those used for prompted writing questions and those available for student notes (called "Post-Its"). The chart for Don shows that in his first work session he read the first 31 of the 43 pages of the *The Landlady*, and only accessed resources on two pages, nine and ten. In his second session, Don skimmed forward to find his place, eventually jumping to page 31 and then finished reading the story. Starting from page 39 he responded to questions, wrote in Post-Its, and accessed a graphic overview of the story's setting and characters. In his final three work sessions Don reread some pages, skimmed through some others, and responded to more of the questions. All together it appears that while Don read the entire story, he did not make much use of available resources, and only answered 4 of the 11 required questions. The action chart for Melinda shows a different strategy. She responded to 9 of the questions, and did so as she read the story, rather than reading first and answering later as did Don. Melinda also made frequent use of the self-monitoring questions and other resources.

There is, of course, no way of knowing solely from this monitor what students were actually doing during each event. Some reasonable conclusions can be drawn however by creating an event data base and then searching and sorting the data in various ways. For example, a search to find just when Don read page 36 of *The Landlady* text begins by selecting from the data base all events transpiring on that page. From this set, some events can be eliminated, such as those where Don accessed a self-monitoring question, since these questions obscure the text. Other events are far too short, only one or two seconds, for Don to have read the page, and so these too can be eliminated. Once all such events have been cleared away, often only one event remains, and it can be marked as the time when Don read page 36 (assuming of course that he did read it). Some events could not be so clearly described. In a this way we marked each event in each database with our interpretation of its meaning by using codes such as R36 and RR36 for reading and rereading page 36, or WPrediction40 for writing an answer to the prediction question on page 40. When this close analysis was complete, we divided each student's transcript into segments of similar reading behavior, and prepared a segment summary which compiled all relevant information. An example is shown in Figure 1. Physical parameters for each segment are shown to the left, and a description, along with event interpretations, is to the right.

With the data for each student displayed and organized in these ways it was possible to construct a detailed view of how these students approached the reading of literature presented in a hypertext environment. From these data we have been able to make two general sets of observations, one with regard to the reading strategies students adopted, and the other about the basic skills students need to successfully function in a hypertext reading environment.

Session 1 53 events 1592 seconds	Read 3-31, accessing resources only on page 9 and 10. R03, R04, R05, R06, R07, R08, R09, WAdvice9, R10?, R11, R12, R13, R14, R15, R16, R17, R18, R19, R20, R21, R22, R23, R24, R25, R26, R27, R28, R29, R30, R31
Session 2.1 25 events 437 seconds	Skimmed to find place. Jumped from 16 to 31. Read 32-38. RR16?, RR31?, R32, R33, R34, R35, R36, R37, R38, R39
Session 2.2 43 events 654 seconds	Studied 39-43 by reading text, responding in popups, writing in PostIts, and accessing overview. WPage1, R40, R41, R42, R43, RR43?, WPostIt40, WAuthor43, RR43?, WPage2

Figure 1: Part of Don's reading of 'The Landlady'

Hypertext Reading Patterns

We observed students using six different reading patterns:
Skimming: Moving through the text at a pace too fast for reading or studying.
Checking: Moving through the text and/or resources systematically, checking things out but apparently but not reading or responding.
Reading: Moving through the text systematically, visiting pages long enough to read the text, but with little or no use of supporting resources.
Responding: Accessing one or more of the interactive resources (self-monitoring questions, popups) and writing responses.
Studying: Moving through the text systematically, visiting pages long enough to read the text and using resources in an integrated manner.
Reviewing: Moving systematically through text which has previously been read, rereading pages and/or revisiting resources.

Two underlying characteristics distinguish these six strategies: interactivity and integratedness. Interactivity is a measure of the degree to which students interact with the reading material. *Skimming* and *Reading* are more passive patterns, with students doing little more than moving from place to place. When *Responding* or *Studying* students are more active, performing more, and more complicated, tasks. In contrast, integratedness relates to the variety, rather than the number, of actions taken by students. *Studying* is the most integrated reading pattern described here because, when studying, students make use of all the hypertext features provided in the stories. The variance of the six reading patterns along these two dimensions is summarized in Figure 2.

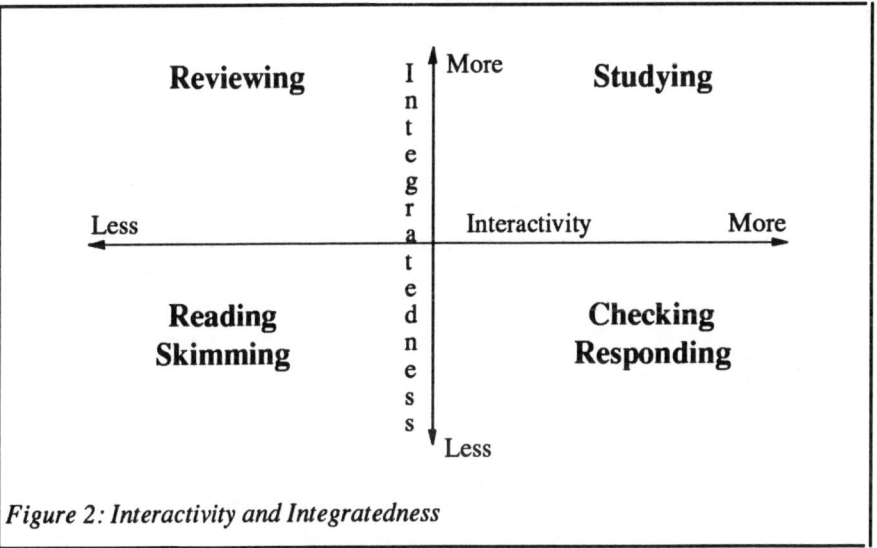

Figure 2: Interactivity and Integratedness

In general we found that students' reading patterns over time became more interactive and more integrative. We identified a variety of possible explanations for these changes. It could be that students came to believe that Studying, the most interactive and integrated pattern, was the most advantageous in completing their task. Alternatively, structural changes in the hypertext features of the stories could have been the cause. In particular, in *Louisa, Please Come Home* the required writing activities were held on resource cards separate from the story text. For *The Landlady*, these prompts were placed directly within the text. Thus, in the first story, students might naturally first read the story and later write their responses, while in the second, it was reasonable to integrate reading and responding within a single visit to each section of the text.

The question of what motivated students to change their reading patterns leads to a final observation about those patterns. In reviewing our data we found little evidence to suggest that these students viewed stories presented in hypertext as anything different from any other assignment: something to be gotten through with as little pain as possible. More than anything else, these reading patterns reflect the choices of students with an assignment completion mentality; a mentality not at all compatible with the philosophy of student control and exploration which underlies the history and development of hypertext. Evidently, more is required to promote actively making a choice, than just having a choice.

Hypertext Skills

Our second set of observations are speculations about the attitudes and skills readers need to exploit properly new hypertext reading environments. We suggest a list of three. First, readers need more than just an introductory understanding of the hardware and software they are operating. Although this seems a perfectly straight forward expectation, we found that sometimes even subtle deficiencies led to substantial difficulties later. For instance, we found it difficult to teach all of our students to reliably transfer their hypertext files between hard and floppy disks. In response, we had them work exclusively from the more secure, but slower, floppies. These slower disks may have robbed the documents of some of the spontaneity and fluidity that is characteristic of, and perhaps critical for hypertext to function effectively.

Second, hypertext readers must be able to erect mental models of the physical structure of documents, as well as the models of document content. In point of fact, this is also a requirement when reading from paper. But hypertext documents are inherently more complicated than paper documents and readers often lack hypertext equivalents of the long established navigational clues and tools provided in books.

Third, and most important, readers must adopt "multi-phasic" reading strategies. That is, the idea that reading requires multiple, distinctive phases of activity in which students "revisit the same content material in a variety of different contexts, with each visit bringing out additional aspects of that content's complexity that are missed in the single pass of linear coverage" (Spiro & Jehng, 1990, p. 163).

Our students did not adopt multi-phasic reading strategies. Nor did they within their experience of these hypertext stories internalize Nelson's grand hypertext vision. None the less, this study does contribute to an ongoing effort to understand just what readers do when they read hypertext. It has served to develop a new set of data collection and analysis techniques. It has identified six reading patterns used by middle school students. It suggests that these reading patterns are not isolated from other features of the reading and instructional environment. Finally, it has given us a body of experience from which to continue the study of hypertext and the new literacy requirements it thrusts upon readers. From such understandings we hope to assist reading teachers and their students join the hypertext revolution and move it from revolt to reality.

Credits. Research reported in this paper was supported in part by the U.S. Department of Education Grant #R215A92116, awarded by the Secretary's Fund for Innovation in Education (FIE).

References

Anderson-Inman, L. (1989). 'Electronic studying: Information organizers help students study "better," not "harder," - Part II'. *The Computing Teacher,* 16(9), 21-29, 53.

Apple Computer, Inc, (1987), *HyperCard* [Computer program]. Cupertino, California

Dahl, R. (1978).' The landlady'. In *The best of Roald Dahl.* New York: Random House.

Enabling Technologies, Inc .(1988). *ElectroText* [Computer Program]. Eugene, Oregon.

Horney, M. A., and Anderson-Inman, L. (1992, April). 'The ElectroText Project: Hypertext reading patterns of middle school students'. Paper presented at the annual conference of the American Educational Research Association, San Francisco, California.

Jackson S. (1988). 'Louisa, please come home'. In K. Robinson (Ed.), *Scope English Anthology, Level 2.* New York: Scholastic, Inc.

Nelson, T. H. (1987). *Literary machines.* South Bend, IN: The Distributors.

Spiro, R. J. & Jehng J. (1990). 'Cognitive flexibility and hypertext: Theory and technology for the non-linear and multidimensional traversal of complex subject matter'. In D. Nix and R Spiro (Eds.), *Cognition, Education, & Multimedia* (pp. 163-205). Hillsdale, New Jersey: Lawrence Erlbaum